SHINING
MOMENTS

SHINING MOMENTS

MOMENTS

STORIES FOR LATTER-DAY SAINT CHILDREN

BY LUCILE C. READING

Salt Lake City, Utah

No part of this book may be reproduced in any
form or by any means without permission in writing
from the publisher, Deseret Book Company,
P.O. Box 30178, Salt Lake City, Utah 84130.
Deseret Book is a registered trademark of
Deseret Book Company.

First printing April 1985
Second printing October 1985
Third printing May 1986
Fourth printing June 1987
Fifth printing August 1988

Library of Congress Cataloging-in-Publication Data

Reading, Lucile C.
    Shining moments.

    Summary: A collection of true stories reflecting
Mormon values.
    1. Children — Religious life.   2. Christian life —
Mormon authors — Juvenile literature.   [1. Mormons.
2. Christian life.   3. Short stories]   I. Title.
BX8656.R4   1985   242'.62   85-1655
ISBN 0-87747-687-X

CONTENTS

FOREWORD

"Whenever you stood in Lucile's presence," said one of her friends, "it was a shining moment."

Perhaps that was because of her capacity to love people and life deeply. She often quoted Emily Dickinson's words: "To have been made alive is so chief a thing. . . . The mere sense of living is joy enough." (George Frisbee Whicher, *This Was a Poet,* University of Michigan Press, 1957, page 14.) Perhaps it was because of her own radiant person: her rich silver hair, her intensely blue and piercing eyes, her soft skin but firm chin, and her finely tapered hands that knew and loved work. She wore blue often—impeccably and rightly groomed.

Lucile Cardon Reading was born in Logan, Utah, to Louis and Rebecca Ballard Cardon. She graduated from Utah Agricultural College (now Utah State University) with highest honors. She went to work in Salt Lake City, Utah, but there discovered that she had tuberculosis. Keith Reading, who married her despite her illness, took her to a family cabin in Logan Canyon and nursed her back to health. They made their home in Centerville, Utah, and two sons were born to them.

In the late fifties Lucile's eyes were failing. At that time few surgeons would dare attempt cornea transplants, but Lucile found a doctor in California who promised success. She patiently endured two cornea transplants and the hours, days, weeks of lying blindfolded with her head sandbagged lest she make a movement before the tissues were healed. At last the bandages were removed and she could open her eyes. From that shining moment, her life changed dramatically.

In the early sixties, Lucile became a member of the editorial board of the *Children's Friend.* One of her first writing assignments was a series of retold true stories entitled "Shining Moments." Lucile said the title occurred to her one Sunday in church from the hymn "Improve the Shining Moments."

The stories she wrote have been described as "spare and lean. Carefully drafted, yet simple in format, these vignettes made gospel truths clear in a rich and varied language that children understood." (*The Friend,* June 1982, page 6.)

Lucile read widely and was a thorough researcher. She had a quick, alert mind that gave her the rare insight to know the moments that would shine—like the pathos of the Indian chief playing "Come, Come, Ye Saints" on his violin. Or the girl who gave up her only doll. Or the boy who loved baseball but chose not to play on his baseball team on Sunday. Lucile, as a member of the Primary General Board, traveled widely and listened to Primary workers, capturing in her stories many of the experiences she heard.

In all of these shining moments there is a pattern—an echo of Lucile's own shining moment on that long-ago day when she opened her eyes and could see, and knew in her heart the goodness of the

Lord. From that moment to the last morning of her life she gladly gave her talents, her gifts, her great strength, everything she had to the service of the Savior. Her stories reflect his goodness, his love for his children, his concern, and his care.

Reading these "Shining Moments" is like standing in Lucile's presence again. She generated warmth, wisdom, hope, and love; and we left her, as Carol Lynn Pearson says, "wearing some of her light." (*A Widening View,* Bookcraft, 1983, page 40.)

MABEL JONES GABBOTT

*Few acts of courage or faith seem
exciting and even fewer are rewarded
with medals, yet every act done quietly
by an everyday boy or girl
scatters shining moments throughout
the lives of those it affects.*

MADELINE'S DREAM

Madeline tucked her clothes under her arm and ran down the stairs and into the kitchen where her mother was preparing breakfast.

Mother looked up to say good morning to her little girl, but when she saw how pale and breathless Madeline was, she asked, "What's the matter? Are you sick?"

"No," answered Madeline, but at that moment she could say no more. She sank down onto a stool near the fireplace and stared at the bright flame. She wondered how she could ever put into words the strange dream she had just had and what her mother would think even if she could.

In her dream Madeline had seen herself as a young lady sitting in a small strip of meadow close to the vineyard. As she watched to make sure the goats did not trample the vines and eat them, she glanced down at the Sunday School book on her lap.

When she looked up again, Madeline was startled to see three foreigners. She shivered in fright, but almost at once a feeling of peace flooded over her as one of the men said, "Don't be frightened. We have come from a place far away to tell you about the true and everlasting gospel."

1

Then the men told Madeline that an angel had directed a boy to find an important book of gold hidden in the earth. They said that some day she would be able to read this book, and afterward she would gladly leave her home, cross the great ocean, and go to America to live.

Now in the warm, sweet-smelling kitchen Madeline relived her dream. It all seemed so real to her that she turned pale again and began to tremble.

When Father came in from milking the goats a few moments later, he asked, just as her mother had done, "What's the matter? Are you sick?"

Madeline could only shake her head.

Father gently stooped beside her, picked up a stocking, and without another word began to help her dress. Afterward he lifted her onto his lap and quietly asked, "Do you want to tell me about it?"

Madeline nodded. It was difficult to get the words started at first, but then they seemed to tumble over each other in their eagerness to be spoken.

Mother left her preparations for their simple breakfast of figs, potatoes, and goat's milk so she could hear every amazing detail of the dream. Father listened intently too, occasionally nodding his head as if he understood more than was being said.

That night as the family gathered around the fireplace for their evening prayer, Father told again the story of why they lived in the small village high in the north Italian Alps.

Their grandparents many generations back had once built homes in the lovely valleys at the foot of these lofty mountains. There they lived simple, happy lives, basing all they did on the teachings of the apostles who had lived at the time of Jesus Christ. The Vaudois (people who live in the valleys of the Alps) even sent forth missionaries two by two to teach, and many people from other lands were converted to their faith.

Before long news of their success reached Rome, and word was sent to the Vaudois valleys that the people must give up their own church and abide by the dictates of the larger ruling church in Rome. This the Vaudois refused to do. Instead they clung with even greater faith to the authority and teachings of the New Testament as handed down to them.

Angered, Pope Innocent VIII proclaimed a general crusade for the extermination of every member of the Vaudois church. Soon the peaceful valleys where they lived were filled with tragedy and destruction. There was hardly a rock that did not mark a scene of death, and those who survived were driven from their homes. They retreated higher and higher up the steep mountains.

The many years of unbelievable suffering that followed resulted in the death of all but three hundred members of the Vaudois church. These people settled high in the Piedmont valleys of the Alps, their villages seeming to cling to the mountainsides surrounded by inaccessible crags and cliffs.

In those early days it was hard to eke out a living. Each spring the women and children went down the steep mountains with baskets and carried the soil that had been washed down in the winter storms back up to their terraced fields and gardens. But in these craggy mountains they were quite isolated, and here they raised their hands to the sky and, as their fathers before them had done, solemnly swore to defend their homes and their religion to the death.

Madeline's family had heard this story many times, but they never tired of it. Even the youngest children thrilled to hear about the courage of their tall, strong grandparents. The older children often expressed gratitude for their home and for the church with its motto "The light shining in darkness."

Long after everyone else had fallen asleep that night, Madeline could hear the murmur of her parents' voices. The last thing she remembered before she went to sleep was hearing her mother insist, "But we already have the true gospel, so there couldn't be any real meaning to that story Madeline told us."

Madeline did not hear Father's answer, but occasionally as the years went by he would question her concerning her dream. Even though some of the details became vague to her, he never forgot them.

About eight years after Madeline's dream, the king of Sardinia, pressured by England and other countries to cease persecuting the Piedmont protestants, granted his Vaudois subjects freedom of religion. The tragic 800-year war ended in February 1848.

The very next year Lorenzo Snow, who later became fifth president of the Church, was called to open a mission in Italy. But he and his two companions could not find anyone interested in their message. Discouraged, Elder Snow wrote, "I see no possible means of accomplishing our object. All is darkness!"

On September 18, 1850, Lorenzo Snow and his two companions climbed a high mountain in northern Italy and on a large projecting rock offered a fervent prayer for guidance. They were then inspired to dedicate the land for the preaching of the gospel, and they named the rock on which they stood the Rock of Prophecy.

Before leaving the mountain, the missionaries sang "The Hymn of the Vaudois Mountaineers in Times of Persecution." The strains of this song had floated down into the valleys many times from high caves and fissures in the rocks where these persecuted people had been hiding. It had been a rallying cry as the Vaudois took up arms to fortify their mountain passes. It had been sung in thanksgiving in their church services. Now the three missionaries standing on the Rock of Prophecy sang the stirring words:

For the strength of the hills we bless thee,
Our God, our fathers' God;
Thou hast made thy children mighty
By the touch of the mountain sod.

One Saturday afternoon shortly afterward Madeline's father went home early from his work of building a chimney for a neighbor. He told his family that three strangers were coming to bring an important message.

"I must dress in my best clothes and go welcome them," he said.

Early Sunday morning he found the men he was looking for and invited them to go home with him. As they walked up over the winding paths and through the dangerously narrow mountain passes, Madeline's father told them about the dream his daughter had had many years before.

When they reached his small rock house, they found Madeline sitting in a little strip of meadow close to the vineyard. She looked up from the Sunday School book she was reading into the faces of the three foreigners. They told her they had come to give her people the message contained in a wonderful book of gold that had been taken out of the earth, and they said that she would be able to read this book.

That evening Madeline's neighbors came to meet the strangers and hear their message. Some of them found it so unusual and exciting that they stayed up all night to learn more about the newly revealed truths brought to them by these missionaries of The Church of Jesus Christ of Latter-day Saints.

Some baptisms were held in October 1850. Twenty families eventually accepted the gospel, and as Madeline's dream became a reality, the Vaudois area truly became "The light shining in darkness."

KURT'S HOME EVENING

Kurt threw himself down on his bed and buried his head tightly in a pillow to hold back the tears. Even when a boy is ten years old, it is sometimes pretty hard not to cry when disappointments come.

Two weeks ago he had asked his mother about holding a family home evening like all the other families he knew were doing. She told him he would have to talk to his dad, and she suggested that it be done rather carefully.

Kurt had thought he was being careful. He had said, as if it did not matter so much, "Dad, all the guys are talking about their family home evenings. Why don't we have one?"

"We don't need anyone to tell us when to talk with our kids," was Dad's reply.

Several nights later while Kurt and his younger brothers and sister sat at the supper table, Dad had looked around and said, "Now this is all the family home evening anyone would want."

That was when Kurt had replied, "But, Dad, other families have a special program with lessons out of the book our home teachers brought. I've read the first lesson and it's keen. Why can't we have a regular home evening?"

Now Kurt remembered that Dad had again said, "We don't need any special lessons. We're together enough!"

Nothing had been said since then until last night when Dad came home from the service station and announced that he did not have anything special to do for a change. Almost without thinking, Kurt said, "Swell, Dad. Let's have a family home evening." He started to add, "All the kids . . . ," but a look from his father silenced him.

A few minutes later Dad said, "I know what we'll do. Let's all get in the car and go over to see Uncle Morris." So they went to visit their uncle. It was fun playing with the cousins while the older folks sat around talking about things which did not matter at all to children.

On the way home Dad said, "Now *that* was a family home evening *my* way."

"Well," Kurt replied, "I'd still like to have the other kind too."

Dad, who was in a good mood, answered, "Okay, son, just to please you, we'll have one your way tomorrow night."

So when Kurt came home from school this afternoon, he got out the book and read the lesson again. He and Mother talked it over, and they asked one of the younger children to pray. Mother baked Dad's favorite kind of cookies, and an air of excitement almost like Christmas was in the home.

As soon as Dad walked in the door, Kurt knew that his father was unhappy. He overheard his dad telling Mother that everything had gone wrong all day and that he was going to bed as soon as he ate supper.

Kurt thrust his head even deeper in the pillow as he remembered how foolish he had been to remind

Dad of his promise the night before. This had only made Dad more tired and more cross. He looked straight at Kurt and said, "I'm sick of your fussing about a home evening. We're not going to have one at all—and let this be the end of it!"

As the tears flowed, Kurt prayed for forgiveness and for help.

Only a few minutes later Kurt heard his dad's footsteps on the stairs. Then he felt a hand on his shoulder, and Kurt knew a moment of sheer joy and gratitude as his father softly said, "Forgive me, son. Let's go downstairs and have that family home evening now. Everyone is waiting for us."

A GIFT FOREVER

It was a cold snow-bright morning. For several hours Hal had been hunting a rabbit for Christmas supper. It was sheer joy to the eleven-year-old boy to be out in the fields, his very own shotgun slung over his shoulder. He stopped frequently to look again at it and to run his fingers lovingly down the barrel.

What a glorious surprise it had been that morning when Dad had handed him a long, brown paper-wrapped package, which Hal immediately opened and found the gun inside. He had wanted one so much he ached, but whenever he had spoken of its possibility as a Christmas gift, Mother had been quick to discourage the hope.

Dad had been sick for a long time, and often there was not enough money for food. How he had managed to get a second-hand shotgun for Hal was a wonderful mystery to the boy.

Suddenly a flutter of motion broke the stillness, and a fat rabbit hopped up in front of Hal and started over a small rise. He took careful aim, and with the first shot from his gun brought down the animal.

As he ran to pick up his kill, he heard someone call, "Hello! Merry Christmas! Come on in!" Hal had been so absorbed in his gun and in the rabbit that he had not noticed a house nearby, but now he saw a tall man standing in a doorway smiling a welcome.

Hal scraped away some snow so his precious gun wouldn't get wet and hung the rabbit in a tree in case a dog might come by. More than anything, he wanted to protect his Christmas gun and his first kill with it.

Once inside the house, the man watched as the boy's eyes slid quickly over the room. Hal had never seen anything like it before. There was a rug on the floor and lace curtains hung at the windows. But better than anything else was a shelf of books near a big stone fireplace where a fire threw heat out into the beautiful room.

"Go over and help yourself to a book," the man invited when he saw how the boy's eyes lighted up. "My wife is fixing us some hot cocoa."

The only book Hal had ever seen before was an old reader from which his mother had taught him to read. Now before him were thirty or more volumes!

He chose one with the title *The Last of the Mohicans*. Without knowing what was happening, he was soon lost in the pages of its story as time stood still. He was finally aroused by a touch on his shoulder and a woman's kind voice saying, "Here's another cup of cocoa to warm you on your way."

"Yes," the man added, "you must start home before dark or your mother will worry."

Hal quickly put the book back on the shelf and hastily gulped down the cocoa. Embarrassed, he managed to mumble his thanks and started toward the door.

The man smiled, took the book back off the shelf, and held it out to the boy. "Put it inside your jacket to keep it dry," he said. "When you've finished, come back and get another."

Mechanically Hal picked up his shotgun outside the door, but he wasn't really thinking about it anymore. Instead his thoughts were all on the book inside his coat and on the promise of other books waiting for him to read.

He was halfway home before he noticed the numbing cold and realized it was late afternoon. That is when he remembered that the rabbit he had been so excited to shoot with his own gun was still hanging in the tree where he had so carefully placed it.

What mattered on that Christmas afternoon was Hal's discovery that there was more thrill and joy in reading a book than there was in owning a shotgun. That was the afternoon that the wonder of a book turned out to be Hal's best Christmas present, and he decided that someday he would write one himself.

THE COAT

Heber shivered in his thin coat as cold November wind whipped around him. All he really wanted for his birthday was a warm coat, but he knew that asking for one would only upset his mother. He remembered how she had cried last Christmas because she did not have enough money to even buy him a stick of candy.

Nine days after he was born, Heber's father had died, and his mother had then moved from the fine house where he had been born to a small one where they lived for many years. The roof leaked, and often on cold nights they went to bed early because there was no coal for heat. Sometimes they even went to bed hungry, for fried bread was not always satisfying food for supper and there was no money for anything else.

There were days and nights when Heber's mother would sew and sew to earn money even though she was too tired to finish a dress for a customer. Then Heber would crawl under the sewing machine and push the pedal up and down so that his mother's tired legs might have a rest from treadling.

As they worked together in the lamplight, over

and over again she would tell him stories of his father, grandparents, Church history, or the scriptures. Then they would plan together for the time when they would have money for coal and food and all the clothes they could wear.

November 22nd dawned clear and cold. "Happy birthday, Heber!" called his mother as she handed him the most beautiful coat Heber had ever seen. It was made of material he had often seen his mother sewing and fit him perfectly. Heber hugged it to himself. He could hardly wait to go out in the cold and feel its warmth about him.

A few weeks later as Heber hurried on an errand, he passed a boy about his size who was shivering with the intense cold of the day. Heber noticed that the boy was wearing only a thin sweater. Heber shivered too even though he had on his warm overcoat.

The boy looked at Heber's coat with such longing that, almost before he knew what he was doing, Heber stopped, took off his coat, and insisted that the boy put it on and keep it.

That afternoon Heber's mother saw him wearing his old coat instead of his new one. "What have you done with your lovely new coat?" she asked.

For just a moment Heber wondered how he could tell her that he had given it away. "Oh, Mother," he blurted out, "I saw a boy who needed it lots worse than I, so I just gave it to him!"

"Couldn't you have given him your old one?" she asked.

Heber J. Grant looked up into her face hoping she would understand. He saw that her eyes were misted with tears, and he threw his arms around her as she gently answered her own question, "Of course you couldn't, Heber," she said. "Of course you couldn't."

THE PERFECT CHRISTMAS PRESENT

In just two weeks it would be Christmas, and Jean had not yet found exactly the right present. She needed something very special for her sister, who had been both father and mother to her since their parents' death. Jean had thought and thought about what she might give. She had looked in the store windows for months, hoping to see something her sister might like.

On this wintry afternoon Jean's nose was pressed against the cold glass as she carefully considered each article in the cluttered window of the small antique shop. It was nearly dusk, and the rays of the setting sun caught and held for a second the shining blue of a string of beads that was almost hidden under other items. The beads reminded Jean of her sister's blue eyes, and she knew she had found the perfect present at last.

Jean pushed open the door to the dingy little shop. "Would you please let me look at that string of blue beads in the window?" she asked the man behind the counter.

He reached into the window and held them up so they again caught the rays of the setting sun.

"Oh," breathed Jean, "they're just perfect. I'll take them."

The man studied the little girl before him as if he did not know quite what to do. Finally he asked, "Are you buying these for someone special?"

Jean's eyes shone with love as she told him how good her sister was to her and then clouded over with sadness as she explained that this was their first Christmas alone because their mother had recently died.

The man listened without comment. "How much money do you have?" he asked when Jean finished her story.

She poured out on the counter all the pennies and nickels and dimes she had been saving for months. "I even emptied my bank," she explained simply. "Do I have enough?"

The man looked down at the price tag on the beads, which was turned toward him and away from Jean. For a moment he seemed unsure about what to do. Then he looked down into the girl's trusting eyes.

"It's enough," he answered, "for you are paying the highest possible price—all that you have. I'll wrap the beads for you."

GEORGE'S BIRTHDAY PRESENT

George was a little boy who lived in Salt Lake City. At that time the temple had not yet been completed and there were few meetinghouses. When boys and girls became eight years old, they were baptized in nearby streams or ponds. All the Cannon children were baptized on their eighth birthday in the Jordan River, which ran near their grandfather's home.

A few weeks before George was to be eight years old, he became very ill with typhoid fever. When his birthday came, George was still too weak to walk. At first, both Father and Mother said they thought he was not well enough to be baptized on his birthday. However, the boy insisted.

"Please, Father," he begged, "take me to the Jordan River in your buggy. If you will carry me down to the river to be baptized, I know I'll be able to walk out afterward by myself."

Father and Mother looked at the eager face of their little boy. They could not question the faith of this child who had been so sick.

It was a beautiful morning, warm and sunny. Father brought the horse and buggy around to the front door. He carried George to it and tucked a light blanket around George's legs. Mother climbed in beside him, and the family drove to the Jordan River.

George J. Cannon often told about the feeling of strength that spread through him after he came up out of the water of baptism: "I walked from the river and ran to the buggy," he would say. "This was a moment I can never forget."

PHILEMON'S FAITH

Some men and boys were stretched out under a large tree in a little grove near Nauvoo. Among them were loyal followers of the Prophet Joseph Smith, but there were also several of his enemies.

A young man by the name of Philemon Merrill rested quietly by the side of the Prophet listening to a large and powerful man boast that he could throw anyone in the group. "In fact," he said, "I can throw anyone in the whole state of Illinois."

Stephen Markham was a bodyguard of Joseph Smith. He was a huge man and noted for his ability to wrestle. He accepted the challenge and, much to everyone's surprise, was quickly thrown.

This only served to whet the appetite of the boaster, who insisted that someone else become his victim. The enemies of the Prophet began to insult him and his followers, calling them cowards because they did not quickly send another man to meet the challenge.

Joseph Smith turned to the young man beside him and said, "Get up and throw that boaster!"

Surprise and fear gripped Philemon. Since he was not a wrestler, he was tempted to refuse; however, the look in the Prophet's eyes stopped him. Joseph Smith's followers knew he was a man of great faith. So strong was his faith that his followers felt they could do anything the Prophet asked of them.

Philemon arose to his feet to obey the strange command given him. As he did so, his body was suddenly filled with unusual strength. He lifted his arms and stood ready for action. Despite the protests of his friends, Philemon even gave the boasting wrestler his choice of sides.

As they began to grapple, the Prophet said, "Philemon, when I count three, throw him!"

Philemon's whole body and soul swelled with an unquestioning faith in his ability to carry out the command of Joseph Smith. As the word *three* was pronounced by the Prophet, the young man with the strength of a giant lifted his large opponent and threw him over his left shoulder while the amazed group watched in silent awe. Then a cheer rang through the little grove.

There were no more challenges to wrestle that day.

WHEN DID YOU STOP?

The boy sat in the principal's office. Occasionally he looked up at his mother. He hoped she would not scold him again or cry, for she looked as if she might at any moment. He dreaded seeing the principal, but at the same time he longed for the visit to be over.

But then what? he wondered. His mother had told him that if this school did not accept him, she was sure no other one would. He was too young to get a job, and he could not just stay home and listen to his mother tell him again how disappointed she was in him. Oh, how he hoped the principal would accept him.

The principal came into the office. The boy had never before seen such a big man, and his bigness seemed more than just physical size. There was something about the man's eyes and the way that his hair was so alive—it almost crinkled as it sprang back from a high forehead. Something made the boy squirm down in his seat so as not to be seen and yet at the same time to sit taller in the chair. It was a very strange feeling.

His mother looked up anxiously at the principal, who smiled kindly at her and nodded understandingly as she told him the problem. She asked that her son might be accepted at the school and helped to learn how to act as well as how to study. She explained in minute detail that the boy had had trouble with all of his teachers and that the school where he had been was glad and relieved to be rid of him.

The boy felt as if the mother's painful recital of his faults would never end. She explained that she knew this was a Church school and that its standards were high, but she hoped it would overlook some of her son's bad habits.

The principal looked at the boy and said he would like to ask a few questions. His clear penetrating gaze made the boy squirm again, and he knew he could never lie to this man no matter how uncomfortable the truth might be.

"Do you smoke?" the principal asked.

He did not even look surprised when the boy, despite the smell of tobacco on his clothes, answered, "No, sir."

"Good," said the principal. "When did you stop?"

The boy met the man's eyes squarely as he replied, "I stopped last night."

The principal put out his hand and smiled as he said, "I believe you, son. You may enter this school, and I'll do everything I can to help you."

The boy held out a hand. It was caught up in the warm grasp of a hand so big that the smaller one seemed lost—lost physically, but feelings of strength and understanding flowed from the man to the boy so they both knew that from this moment the boy would live up to the trust placed in him by David O. McKay, the principal of Weber Stake Academy.

BE OF GOOD FAITH

It was storming outside, and the only sound in the cabin was Father's voice quietly explaining why he had given flour to those who had come by during the day. There was much sickness in the little community, and a mixture of flour and water seemed to be the best possible medicine.

Patiently Father reminded the children that they had been especially blessed because none of them had contracted the strange "winter sickness." Even though the crops had failed in the fall, it had been possible for him to trade flour for the wagons he made for his neighbors or for pioneers going through Fillmore on their way to the west coast.

Early that morning Mother said, "Please don't give away any more flour, Father. There's only enough left for a little bread for our own children."

Before Father could answer, a knock came at the door. A neighbor stood outside. He said he needed some flour for his sick wife. Even the youngest child was touched by the look of gratitude on the neighbor's face when Father filled a cup with flour, gave it to him, and said, "Be of good faith. The Lord will provide."

A few minutes later another knock was heard, and a young man hurried in when Father opened the door. The family knew Father could not refuse help when the worried young father said, "Oh, Brother Carling, my baby is dying! I must have some flour."

After the young man left with the flour, Mother started to cry. Father gently put his arm around her and suggested that the family kneel with him in prayer. A feeling of peace and hope came into the little cabin as Father expressed thanks for health, for warmth, and for safety on such a cold November day. Then he prayed that in some way it might be possible for them and their neighbors to get food, especially some flour.

After the prayer, Father asked Mother if she would try to scrape together enough flour from the box to make a little gravy. To her surprise, there was plenty for gravy with some still left over.

While the family was eating, another knock was heard at the door. The man standing outside said he needed services of a good wagoneer and had been told that Father might be able to help. "I have twenty tons of flour here," he said. "I wonder if I could trade flour for wagons."

THE PUMPKIN AND THE BULL

Wilford was busily feeding his father's horned cattle, among which was a ferocious and greedy bull. Wilford fed the big bull first and then placed a pumpkin far out of the reach of this animal so their gentle cow might have her share of food.

In a flash, the selfish bull left his own nearly eaten pumpkin, snatched the one given to the cow, and took off with it.

Wilford, trying to help the hungry cow and irritated at the behavior of the bull, quickly scooped up the pumpkin the bull had left, forgetting that his father had often warned him never to do anything to upset this particular animal.

The angry bull charged. Wilford started to run but stumbled. For one delirious moment he thought that he would be crushed to death or gored by the horns.

With silent but mighty prayer, he hugged the ground, letting the pumpkin roll away from him. With the fury of a tiger, the bull jumped over the boy, plunged his horns into the pumpkin, and tore it to shreds while Wilford scrambled safely over the wooden fence.

"Undoubtedly, he would have done the same thing to me if I had not fallen to the ground," said Wilford Woodruff in telling the story. "This escape, like all others, I attribute to the mercy and goodness of God."

THE COUNT OF THREE

Tomas Perez and his Red Flagger bandit followers rode boldly into the Mormon settlement of Colonia Dublan in Mexico. They demanded a place to sleep and feed for fifty horses.

Early the next morning four of the men captured Anson B. Call, bishop of the settlement, ordered a mule to be saddled for him, and rode off with him to a nearby Mexican village.

The year was 1915, and the Call family had recently returned with a handful of others to Colonia Dublan to help save some of the property of the Latter-day Saints who had been driven from the area during the revolution of 1912. Before their return, Anthony W. Ivins, counselor to President Heber J. Grant, told Bishop Call that he might have to endure many severe trials, but his enemies would not have the power to take his life.

Perez and his bandits rode with their captive for several days. Finally one night they stopped at a house where they all slept for a few hours. After midnight they kicked the Mormon leader awake and told him he was to be killed. They took him about two hundred yards from the house and ordered him to stand before a big cottonwood tree. The Red Flaggers stood only six or eight feet away and cocked their guns as their leader counted.

"One."

Back at Colonia Dublan the settlers had fasted and were praying for the safe return of Bishop Call. His family too knelt in prayer.

"Two."

Bishop Call remembered the promise made to him by President Ivins. How would this promise be kept, he wondered. Yet he knew that somehow it would be, even though he seemed just moments away from eternity. He prayed as he had never prayed before while he waited for the count of three. But instead of the word which would mean his death, out of the darkness came a question from Perez.

"What would you give us to save yourself? Come, we will ride back to Colonia Dublan and see if you are worth 200 pesos to your family and your people."

The cocked rifles were lowered. The bandits and the bishop rode back to the settlement, where grateful settlers gave all they had to prevent the fatal count of three!

THE VISIT

Susan sat on the edge of her high narrow bed watching the other children in the convalescent ward of a large London hospital. They were gathered at one end of the room dressing their dolls, playing games, and talking together. In her arms Susan held a small worn doll.

Every day was the same. After the parents left the hospital with promises to return, leaving behind little gifts of love, the children gathered at the end of the room to relive the visits, to show their gifts, and to talk excitedly about plans to go home—all but Susan. The children left her alone.

Susan's mother was dead, and her father had been to see her just once in many long weeks. He stayed only a few minutes. There was no gift, no promise of a return visit, and no talk of going home. She had no gifts to share—nothing but the little old doll she brought with her, and even the girls didn't want that.

When the children talked of their visitors, Susan had nothing to say. Day after day she sat on her bed quiet and sad and filled with longing to join the group. Every night she prayed that her father or someone might come to visit her.

It had been an especially lonely day. Late in the afternoon Sir William Osler, one of the great physicians of all time, walked into the room and went straight to Susan's bed. He smiled at her and then said in a voice loud enough for all the children to hear, "May I sit down please?"

Susan's eyes lit up with welcome and excitement. "I can't stay very long this time," Dr. Osler went on, "but I've wanted so much to come and visit with you. I haven't had a chance to do so before."

Susan could not know that Dr. Osler had looked into the room earlier that day and had seen her alone on the bed while all the other children were playing together. He had asked a nurse about her.

"We've tried to get Susan to play," the nurse had answered, "but the other children won't have anything to do with her. Children are strange. If you don't have visitors, they think something is wrong with you, and they leave you alone."

Dr. Osler bent over Susan's bed and asked if he might see her doll. He handled it carefully, commented on how precious it was, and even pulled out his stethoscope to listen to its chest. He handed it back to Susan and whispered something the children could not hear.

After a brief visit he started to leave. There was a twinkle in his gentle eyes as he walked away. Then he turned back and said, "I'll see you again soon, Susan. You won't forget our secret, will you? Remember not to tell anyone."

Susan's smile was radiant as the other children, curious and admiring, clustered about her bed to look at her doll and to ask about her famous visitor.

THE LIGHT

The wood lay in complete darkness except for a small glow from the shaded lamp on Jean's bicycle handle. In the summer this was a beautiful place with carpets of flowers and the sun shining through the high trees, but on this moonless night it was impossible to see more than a few feet ahead.

Jean was on her way to visit her grandmother who lived in a small country village near London. She was even more frightened of the darkness this night than of the bombs that might fall at any moment. The time was during the world war. England feared nightly bombings, and by law no bright lights could be used at any time during the night.

Jean imagined that the sky was full of swooping bats and that dark figures moved behind each tree. Her throat was dry, and her hands tightly clenched the handle bars as she pedalled furiously through the night.

Two miles away lay the main coastal road and Jean prayed with all her heart that she might reach it safely. Just as she did so, a strong cold wind almost took her breath away. As it snuffed out the small lamp on her bicycle handle, blackness closed in.

The next mile was all uphill. Ordinarily Jean would have walked most of the way pushing her bicycle, but now she was so frightened that she did not dare dismount. Instead she lay flat over the handle bars and pedalled with all her might, praying as she did that she might be safe and that somehow she might be able to see her way.

This is how Jean Farbus tells the rest of her story:

It was so black all around me that I even began to wonder whether I'd lost my sight. And then suddenly over the brow of the hill appeared a bright glow, the kind of light one gets from the undimmed headlights of an oncoming vehicle. I didn't question their unguarded brilliance in a land under strict blackout curfew but pedalled madly toward them, hoping they wouldn't be too quick in coming over the horizon and then passing to leave me once more a prisoner of the night. They didn't. The light remained constantly in front of me for the rest of my journey.

What was the light? Well, if you know as I do that our Heavenly Father answers prayers, you'll know that he heard my plea that night.

PUMPKIN TITHING

One day while Elder LeGrand Richards was Presiding Bishop of the Church, he met a young boy
carrying a large, odd-shaped pumpkin. Bishop Richards asked the boy what he planned to do with his
pumpkin.

"I'm going to give it to my bishop as tithing on the
crop I have raised all by myself," the boy replied.

Bishop Richards asked the boy's name and com-
mended him for his generous action. He then visited
with him a moment, talking about the importance of
tithing. He explained that blessings come to those
who pay their tithing because they are sharing with
others.

A few days later as Bishop Richards was leaving
the regional storehouse in Salt Lake City to return to
his office, he saw an old couple loading their small
wagon. They were getting ready to take home the
supplies they had just received from the storehouse.
Looking closer, Bishop Richards saw the boy's pumpkin in their wagon. Its huge size and odd shape made
it impossible to mistake. He decided to stop for a
while to chat with the couple before going on.

A short time later the boy was surprised when he

received a letter from Bishop Richards telling him of the joy his pumpkin had brought to this grateful old couple. Now they could have something special for their holiday dinner because a young boy had shared his blessings by paying tithing.

A VOICE FROM THE MIST

As John started down the hill toward home, fog mixed with smoke rolled over him in smothering waves. The frightened ten-year-old boy sat down to try to light the lantern Mr. West had loaned him to use in just such an emergency, but the dampness blew out the flame of the matches. John stood up, pulled his oilskin coat tighter about him, and tried to see ahead through the fog and darkness of the late afternoon.

Earlier that day John's mother had sent him with a basket of food to the home of an old shepherd who lived alone about three miles northeast of Milnthorpe, England, where John lived with his family. It was the first time Mother had ever let John go on this errand alone, and he was both proud and excited. But he had stayed at Mr. West's home too long, and when a dark cloud blacked out the sun before a soft rain started, John jumped up quickly and said goodbye to his old friend.

Mr. West offered to walk back with the boy to Milnthorpe, but John shook his head. "This is my first trip alone," he explained, "and my mother wouldn't let me come alone again if you had to take me home."

35

Now John wished that he had let Mr. West come with him. He imagined all kinds of strange sounds and movements in the fog that closed in around him. He had no idea where he was. Suddenly he came to a big iron gate that marked the end of the road, and from beyond the gate came the frightening growl of a dog.

John was almost paralyzed with fright. Then he remembered that his mother had said that God was always near even though John might sometimes think that he was all alone.

The boy dropped down on his knees and prayed for help. As he did so, all his fear left. He was not surprised a few minutes later to hear a voice call out of the mist, "Johnny, I've come to take you home." It was Mr. West!

The young boy was John Taylor. Although he lived to be eighty years old, he never forgot the quick answer to his prayer as a frightened boy on that lonesome foggy evening.

ME HAVE THANKSGIVING

John was lost. Snow had begun falling soon after he had started through the woods on his way to the store in the small pioneer settlement for the molasses his mother needed to make pies for Thanksgiving dinner. It covered the path, so he had made a wrong turn and had been going around in circles for what seemed like hours.

John knew there was little chance that anyone else would be in the cold, silent, snow-filled woods. Only a few people lived in the pioneer settlement toward which he had started walking, and his family lived miles from any other neighbors. For a moment the boy was filled with fear that was almost panic.

Suddenly a tall man stood before him, an Indian with a gun.

"Please help me," John cried. "I'm lost."

The Indian did not speak a word but picked John up, boosted him onto broad shoulders, and carried him for several miles. Neither spoke.

At first John was frightened, but then he remembered how friendly an Indian mother had been last summer when she had stopped at their home with her sick baby.

"Bring your baby in, and my mother will make it well," John had told her. And his mother had done just that, giving the child medicine and care. Several times afterward the Indian mother had returned with the baby, who was given not only medicine but food and baths and clean clothes. Soon the baby was well again.

The big Indian carried John to a warm tent and put him down. Sitting beside the fire was the baby and the Indian mother who had come to John's home many months before. They smiled at John, and the woman seemed excited as she spoke to the man, although the boy could not understand what was said.

After a while the Indian nodded and then lifted John up and went out into the storm. Again carrying the boy on his shoulders, he tramped through the heavy snow.

Now John had no fear at all.

It was getting dark, and his mother was worried about her son. He should have returned long ago with the molasses. She was looking anxiously out into the storm when the Indian and the boy came to the doorstep. She threw open the door to welcome them both into the house, but the Indian shook his head.

"My squaw and my papoose you helped last summer. Me have thanksgiving here," he said as he laid his hand over his heart. Then he turned and seemed to melt away into the stormy night.

LUTIE'S MAMA

Lutie ran from the house without looking back. She did not stop until she was safely hidden behind the barn, and then she threw herself down on the ground to sob out her grief.

When Papa had told her that Mama was dying, Lutie had begged him to offer a prayer for her mother's recovery. She knew it would help, for many times in the past few years when Mama had been very ill his prayers had made her better. Lutie had said to him, "Papa, I don't want my mama to die. I want you to lay hands upon her!" But he had only shaken his head.

At the thought, Lutie felt another sob come up into her throat and almost choke her.

After she had cried out all the tears that were in her, Lutie finally wiped her eyes and sat up. Then she began to pray. In all of her twelve years, Lutie had never prayed as hard for anything as she prayed now that Papa would be wrong and that Mama would be made well again.

Lutie did not know until long afterward that at the very same time Papa too was on his knees asking a blessing for all the family—but especially for his daughter so that she would be comforted and have courage to accept whatever happened.

Almost an hour went by before Lutie heard Papa calling all the children together. She hesitated only a moment before joining them. Her steps were steady, and she felt a great peace as she walked toward the house. As she had prayed behind the barn, there had come to her something that seemed almost as if a voice had spoken inside of her saying that, even though Mama could not get better, everything would be all right for everyone.

Lutie found all the children gathered about Mama's bed to say a final goodbye to her. Heber, who was just barely five, was sobbing out his grief. Lutie took him in her arms and calmly said, "Don't weep, Heber. Since we went out of this room, I have come to know that in the death of Mama the will of the Lord shall be done."

LET'S PRAY

The Decker family was living on a ranch in Arizona. Many times Inez had coaxed her parents to let her accompany her twelve-year-old brother, Louis, at least once to watch the sheep. Finally her mother said she could go.

Mother packed an especially good lunch, and at sunrise the children left, carrying a book to read and games to play if the long day dragged.

Louis thought it was fun having company, and Inez was as excited as if she were going on a picnic instead of just helping her brother.

The morning passed quickly, and just before noon the two children started after the sheep that were grazing over a little knoll. As they walked, a chilling shriek suddenly ripped through the air as the startled children saw six Apache Indians riding toward them.

Inez began to cry. Louis grabbed the gun, which was always nearby, put his arm bravely around his little sister, and whispered in her ear, "Don't let the Indians know how frightened we are."

Trembling, Inez replied, "Let's pray."

After a short fervent prayer, the children breathlessly waited. With no outward sign of fear, they refused the Indians' demand for either the gun or a sheep. Instead they offered their lunch, which the Apaches took and silently ate, and then watched the Indians mount their horses and ride away.

A PIECE OF BREAD AND JAM

The little girl took a bite out of the bread and jam she held in her right hand and looked at the one she held in her left. How could it work just like magic, she wondered. But Father had promised her that it would, so she decided to try it and see.

Earlier in the day she and the other children had had such fun running and playing together. But then some of the children were called to their homes, and she and one boy were left alone to finish the game.

Suddenly the happy sounds of laughter changed into ones of quarreling, and the boy pushed her down. When she started to cry, he only pulled a face at her and then ran away.

The girl went into the house to find Father as she always did when any trouble came. She had not really been hurt, but it was always comforting to have Father pick her up, wipe away her tears, and talk with her about her problem.

This time as she told him how the boy had pushed her and then run away without waiting to see if she were hurt or helping her up, Father gently wiped away her tears. He listened intently as she also suggested that he immediately go outside with her, find the boy, and severely punish him.

"If I do that," he explained, "then both you and I would have an enemy. But if you went into the pantry, spread some jam on two pieces of bread, took them outside, and gave one of them to the boy who pushed you down, it would work just like magic to help make you friends again. Then rather than being his enemies, you and I would have made a new friend. Try it."

Now she was doing just what her father, Count Leo Tolstoy, had suggested. As she stood in the yard slowly eating her bread and jam, she saw the boy watching her. He started coming toward her and then stopped. She held out the bread. He hesitated a minute, then ran toward her and took it.

The boy and girl smiled at each other as they sat down together to enjoy the sweetness of a piece of bread and jam—and a special moment of friendship.

THE CHRISTMAS SHOPPERS

The stores were gay with the glitter of Christmas. They were filled with exciting games and gadgets and with warm and appealing clothing to tempt Timmy, age nine, and his seven-year-old brother, Billy, who were doing their Christmas shopping with Mr. Smith.

They had gone from store to store looking at many possible gifts and then always shaking their heads when a clerk asked if she could help them. Billy had almost bought a game he wanted, and Timmy had paused an unusually long time before a display of books. But after whispered consultation with each other, the boys decided in each case to look further.

Finally Mr. Smith impatiently asked, "Well, where would you suggest we look next?" He was a member of the club that each year helped to provide Christmas gifts for poor families. He had given Timmy and Billy each four dollars and taken them shopping for gifts they especially wanted.

"Could we go to a shoe store, sir?" asked Timmy. "We'd like a pair of shoes for our dad. He hasn't any to wear when he gets better and goes back to work."

When they reached the shoe store, Billy pulled

something out of his pocket and handed it to Timmy, who smoothed a crumpled piece of paper before giving it to the clerk and explaining that it was a pattern of their father's foot. They had carefully drawn it while he slept in a chair one evening.

The clerk studied the pattern thoughtfully and then walked away. He returned in a few minutes, held out a box containing a pair of shoes, and asked, "Will these do?"

The shoes were so beautiful that the boys almost held their breath. Then Timmy saw the price on the box. "But we only have $8.00," he said in a voice choked in disappointment, "and these shoes are $16.95."

The clerk cleared his throat. "They were," he answered, "but they're on special today for boys who are looking for Christmas gifts. They'll cost you just $3.98, and then you'll have money left over to buy something for yourselves."

"Not for us," the boys exclaimed, "but we can get something for our mother and our two little sisters. Thank you! Oh, thank you, sir!"

Over the boys' heads, the clerk and Mr. Smith exchanged meaningful looks. But Timmy and Billy, excited at being able to buy presents for their parents and sisters, paid no attention to the men. They could hardly wait to finish their Christmas shopping.

NIGHT RIDE

Nearly everyone in the coach was asleep. A little girl, her eyes closed, sat listening to the sounds of the train as it rushed through the soft spring night. She heard too the noise of sleeping passengers and the restless stirring of those in the car who could not seem to get comfortable.

Suddenly her keen ears caught another sound. Someone was crying. Then there came the murmur of voices. Soon afterward an excited woman hurried down the aisle of the car. She bent over each sleeping passenger and asked in a loud whisper, "Are you a minister?"

Finally she called out, "A woman back here wants a prayer. Is there a preacher in this car?"

No one answered; no one offered to help.

The little girl waited until the woman was near her seat. Then she reached up a small hand to stop her and said, "I can pray. Will I do?"

By this time the woman was desperate. "Follow me," she answered. "I guess you're better than no one."

"You'll have to take my arm," replied the girl, "I can't see."

The woman took the hand of the little blind girl and led her to the end of the car. She explained that the woman who was in the ladies' lounge had a great sorrow, that she couldn't stop crying, and that she had asked for a prayer.

"And," confessed the woman, "I don't know what to say to comfort her. I've forgotten how to pray."

The crying woman did not hear the woman and the little girl until they were by her side. She looked up through her tears as she saw a child's hand reach out for hers.

Then a sweet voice began, "Our Father which art in heaven . . ."

When the prayer was finished, the tearful woman wiped her eyes and stood up. There were tears now in the eyes of the other woman too. The little girl smiled at them both. Even though she could not see, she knew they smiled back at her.

HE TOOK HIM BY THE HAND

Eleven-year-old John Roothoof lived in Rotterdam, Holland. He had once been happy going to school and church, playing with his friends, and doing all the things a boy enjoyed. Then without warning, a painful eye disease caused him to lose his sight. No longer could he go to school or read. He could not even see well enough to play with his friends. Each day was filled with darkness and suffering.

Word reached the Latter-day Saints in Holland that President Joseph F. Smith was coming to visit them. John thought about this for a long time, and then he said to his mother, "The prophet has the most power of any man on earth. If you'll take me with you to the meeting so he can look into my eyes, I believe I'll be healed."

At the close of the meeting the next Sunday, President Smith went to the back of the small chapel to greet the people and shake hands with each one. Sister Roothoof helped John, his eyes bandaged, go with the others to speak to their beloved leader.

President Smith took the blind boy by the hand and then with great tenderness lifted the bandages and looked into John's pain-filled eyes. The prophet blessed John and promised him he would see again.

Arriving home, John's mother took the bandages from his eyes so she could bathe them as the doctors had told her to do. As she did so, John cried out with joy. "Oh, Mamma, my eyes are well. I can see fine now—and far too. And I can't feel any pain!"

PETER'S SONG

Peter looked around the strange hospital room. This was the first night in his life he had ever been away from his mother and father, and he was frightened even though the nurses had promised they would be close by.

The doctor too had been especially kind. He had spent a long time trying to explain in language a little boy could understand just what he planned to do in the operation scheduled for Peter early the next morning.

The hospital was a large one, but it was crowded with sick people. The only bed available for Peter was in a little room at the end of the men's ward.

The thought of all the sick men in the big room just outside his door was frightening. He did not want to cry, and for a moment he did not know just what to do. Then Peter pulled the bed sheet right up around his chin and began to pray with all his might that somehow he could stop feeling so awfully afraid and alone.

When Peter finished his prayer, there came into his mind a song he often sang with his friends in Sunday School that began, "Jesus loves me, this I know . . ."

The words had always made Peter feel good, but this night they had such a special meaning for him that he thought he would burst if he did not let them out. He began to sing very softly at first and then with growing enthusiasm.

A nurse going by the door heard a small clear voice swell with the chorus of the familiar song. The words, sung in a sweet, childlike soprano, could be heard all through the men's ward.

The men stopped their talking, turned off their radios, and listened quietly. Tears ran down the cheeks of some of them as they heard the comforting assurance of a little boy singing, "Jesus loves me . . ."

And when Peter finished, he snuggled down in his bed, turned over, and went to sleep. He was not lonely or frightened anymore.

SOMETHING TO DRINK

The boy tossed and turned with fever. His mother had tried in every way she knew to make him more comfortable, but George Albert hurt all over and was almost too weak to raise his head.

He remembered how his mother had told him that once there had been two other children in the family, but both of them had died. He wondered if he were going to die too. Somehow he knew that his mother was wondering the very same thing.

There were few doctors at the time in Salt Lake City where George Albert lived, but his mother was able to get one to come to the house to tell her what was wrong with her boy and how to help him. The doctor said the boy had typhoid fever, which was a hard disease to cure in those days. He said George Albert was very ill and that even after he began to get better, he would have to stay in bed for at least three weeks. The doctor told Mrs. Smith that in the meantime, her son was to have no solid food but needed to drink a large quantity of liquids. The doctor suggested that she brew some coffee to give to the sick boy every little while.

George Albert had been taught that in the Word

of Wisdom given by the Lord to Joseph Smith, all Latter-day Saints were advised not to use coffee. George Albert said he would drink a lot of water instead of coffee and asked him mother to send for Brother Hawks, a ward teacher who called at their home each month.

Brother Hawks worked at the foundry, but since word had come to him that the Smith home needed his help, he hurried over to them as soon as he could get away.

Mrs. Smith told him of the doctor's suggestion about coffee. She told him that George Albert said he did not want to drink any coffee, but he knew that if Brother Hawks would give him a blessing he would get well.

Brother Hawks looked down at the feverish boy, who tossed uncomfortably on his bed. Then he placed his hand on the child's hot forehead and gave him a blessing and promised him that he would be well again very soon.

Early the next morning George Albert opened his eyes. He stirred in the bed, which felt cool and comfortable to him. He called his mother to tell her he felt fine and to ask if he could get up. A few days later when the doctor called at the Smith home to see his patient, he found him outside playing.

George Albert Smith often told the children of the Church the story of his recovery from typhoid fever.

THE CHILDREN'S PRAYER

The afternoon had been filled with laughter and happy play, but then Brother Joseph hurried into the house and told Father that some wicked men were trying to find and harm him. A few minutes later some of Father's friends also came to the door, and the children heard Father tell Mother that they would stay all night to act as guards.

After that even the games that were usually their favorites had not seemed fun to the children.

Now they were holding a meeting in Mother's bedroom with several of their playmates to decide what they could do to help. The children loved Brother Joseph. He always had a smile for them and often stopped to talk as he walked around the streets of Kirtland, Ohio. They wanted so much to help him even though the oldest was just ten and the youngest only four years old.

"I know what we can do," said a seven-year-old girl. "We can pray and ask our Father in heaven to keep Brother Joseph safe from harm."

Just as she said this, Mother passed by the partly opened door and heard the suggestion. Quickly she went to the room where the men were talking and whispered something to Brother Joseph. He excused himself and went with her to the bedroom door.

He arrived just in time to see the children kneel together and hear their simple prayer for his safety. Tears filled his eyes and then rolled down his cheeks as the children rose from their knees by the bedside and one of them said, "I know Brother Joseph will be safe now. The wicked men can't hurt him at all."

Brother Joseph wiped his eyes and returned to the room where he had been sitting with Father and his friends. He told the men who had come to guard him through the night that they could go to their own homes, for he knew that the prayers of the children would be heard. He said he could lie down and sleep in peace without the least fear of being molested.

In the morning the happy children had breakfast with their beloved Prophet Joseph Smith.

SAVED BY THE GREAT SPIRIT

A small party of pioneers traveling from Arizona to Mexico stopped one evening in 1885 near Fort Apache to rest. They were weary from the heat and dust of the desert, especially the women and small children. Added to their weariness was a haunting fear of Geronimo, the chief of the Apaches, and his band of braves, who were killing all whites who crossed their path.

At bedtime the pioneers knelt together around the campfire to thank their Father in heaven for the safety of the day and to ask him to guide them so that with courage and faith they would reach their new home.

As they knelt, a little Indian dog came running into camp, barking and sniffing the ground, and brought a chilling fear to every heart. When the prayer was ended, some of the men of the party slipped noiselessly away to see where the owner of the dog might be. In a clearing nearby were some Indians talking earnestly and occasionally stopping to point toward the camp. As the men breathlessly watched, they saw the braves nod in agreement and then mount their horses and ride away.

With grateful hearts, the party left the campsite the next morning and finally reached Mexico in safety.

A short time later one of the Indians who had been with Geronimo's band told how the plan had been to kill this party of Mormon pioneers, but they could not do so when they found all the members of the camp kneeling in prayer.

They did not know why, but the Great Spirit stayed their hands.

THE SPECIAL FISHING TRIP

The summer was almost over when one Saturday morning Dad said, "I know a fishing hole I think I'll visit this afternoon. Do you boys have anything special planned for today?"

The boys' eyes lighted up in happy anticipation, and right after lunch they all started for Willow Creek.

When they reached the stream, Dad turned off the main gravel road onto a steep dirt one. The road was narrow and full of curves but finally widened out along the creek bank.

After Dad helped the boys untangle their lines and bait their fishhooks, he went a short distance downstream to find a good fishing hole.

James and Joseph did not notice that the sun had clouded over until a loud clap of thunder startled them. With a sudden wild gust of wind, heavy rain began to fall. They hurried back to the car, wet and frightened.

Soon Dad opened the door, climbed inside, and said cheerfully, "Guess we better be starting for home!"

The downpour of rain had turned the dirt road into a sea of mud. Dad tried to plow through it, but the wheels began to spin out of control. Each spin edged the car closer to the embankment.

The anxious moments ticked slowly by while they all thought of their warm, comfortable home. Father suggested that the boys kneel on the seats of the car while they all prayed for help.

The rain continued to splatter the windows of the car until it seemed as if the car were on an isolated island. But soon, above the noise of the pelting storm, they heard the roar of a motor and saw a four-wheel-drive jeep come into view.

The jeep pulled up alongside the stalled car, and a man jumped out. It was an answer to prayer when he called, "We knew someone needed help in this storm!"

WATCHING THE WORLD OUTSIDE

Snow swirled around the little frame house where Mary Ellen lived, and the cold December wind whistled as if trying to get inside. Mary Ellen had been injured when she was born, and her legs had never grown strong enough for her to walk on them.

Each day while her brother and sisters were at school, Mary Ellen sat in front of the window watching the world outside and waiting for them to come home. Although she was nearly twelve, she was less than three feet tall. Mary Ellen did not own a book; she had no radio to listen to or television to watch.

Six years before, Mary Ellen's home had burned down. Nothing had been saved from the fire except the clothes the family had on at the time. Then six months ago all the men in the town had gone on strike, and Father had had no work since. Every day her father grew more silent and looked more worried.

Although it was only a week until Christmas, there had been no holiday preparations. How Mary Ellen prayed that someone would remember them. She thought about what she would like most of all if she had the choice of a gift and decided it would be a record player and a few records of her very own that she could play during the long lonely days.

Across the valley some Primary boys and girls listened as their teacher told of the joy of sharing Christmas with others less fortunate than themselves. They remembered hearing their parents mention how dreary Christmas might be for the families of the men who were on strike in the neighboring town.

"Wouldn't it be exciting," they said, "to bring Christmas joy to one of these families!" They began to plan how they could do so.

Early on Christmas morning as Mary Ellen lay waiting for someone to help her out of bed, she prayed again that, even though they might have no other gifts, there would be food enough for all.

Just then there was a knock at the door. As her family opened it, Mary Ellen heard their exclamations of surprise. No one was in sight, but on the doorstep were gifts of various kinds and shapes and a box heaped high with food. And, wonder of wonders, right in the middle of everything was a record player for Mary Ellen and some records!

As she reached out for them, a shining radiance lighted her face. Such a warm glow was in her heart all that day that it surely must have reached across the snowy Salt Lake Valley to the Primary children and their teacher who helped to make Christmas a very special day for Mary Ellen.

MIRACLE ON THE PLAINS

Early one morning Jane Grover, Grandfather Tanner, and his little granddaughter left their pioneer camp near Council Bluffs, Iowa, to gather wild gooseberries. Grandfather tired easily and soon went back to the wagon to rest, but the girls found many green juicy berries and stayed to fill their buckets.

Suddenly wild shrieks split the quiet morning air. Racing to the wagon, the girls were horrified to see a group of Indians stripping off Grandfather's clothes. They had taken his watch and knife and were trying to drive off the horses.

One Indian grabbed the smaller girl, who started crying in fright. Another lunged at Jane and tried to roughly drag her away with him. Struggling to free herself, she gasped out a short and fervent prayer for help.

Almost instantly Jane experienced a power far beyond anything she had ever known. Calmly she began speaking in a tone of voice that made the Indians drop their captives and stop to listen. In complete amazement, they heard this young girl talking in their own language, begging them to remember the Great Spirit who would not want them to harm their white friends.

Grandfather and the little girl were speechless with surprise. None of their party knew any words of this strange tongue, yet here was Jane speaking with ease and with authority as if she had known it all her life.

The Indians nodded their heads and gave back the watch, knife, and clothes they had taken. Then they shook hands with all and rode quietly away.

Jane's prayer of faith had been answered in an unusual and thrilling way.

ONE SMALL BUCKET

It was a hot dusty July day on the Great Plains. Molly brushed the sticky wet hair back from her forehead and sighed. Every muscle in her body ached with weariness, and her eyes were strained from trying to find some sign along the trail that Brigham Young's party had gone ahead.

The wagon train going west that included Molly and her family had traveled slowly because nearly 600 wagons were in the party and each one was heavily loaded with people, bedding, and supplies.

Trying to follow the trail of President Brigham Young and his company of first pioneers had proved discouraging. Often the train had to stop to make a new road because the changing quicksands of riverbeds had washed out what might have been used before. Sometimes there were seemingly impassable places, and crude bridges had been built over streams and gulleys.

That afternoon as the train stopped to make camp for the night on the bank of a fork of the Platte River, Molly sat down to rest and secretly wipe away an unhappy tear. "I don't believe we'll ever find President Young and President Kimball and all the others,"

65

she told her mother. "I think we must have lost their trail."

"We'll find them," Mother comforted her, "but we must be cheerful and patient."

Not long afterward, just as Molly and her mother were finishing their supper preparations, they heard a glad shout and saw one of the men of the company running toward camp swinging something shiny in his hand.

"Hurrah," he called. "I've found a bucket, and it's the very one that I gave to President Heber C. Kimball before he left Winter Quarters. Now we know we're on the right trail. Hurrah!"

Molly touched the bucket. It looked beautiful to her. She could hardly believe that here on the Great Plains where land stretched hundreds of miles in every direction, with rivers and knolls and grass and sand, one small bucket could be found to mark the trail and show the wagon train the way the first pioneer party had gone.

That night as the members of her wagon train gathered around the campfire for a prayer before sleeping, Molly's sweet young voice joined thankfully in the words of a favorite Mormon song: "All is well! All is well!" The assuring words floated out across the lonely plains.

A SPECIAL DOG

Donnie wished with all his heart that he could have a dog. He often watched his playmates running and playing with their pets.

His father had carefully explained how difficult it would be for the boy to have a dog, but he had promised that, if they ever found just the right one, they would try and buy it. The longing for a pet grew with the boy. He was sure even his father couldn't understand how hard it was to wait for a special dog.

One day Donnie saw a man putting up a sign that said PUPPIES FOR SALE and asked about them. The man who owned the dogs liked Donnie at once. He seemed to feel there was something special about the boy although he could not decide just what it was.

"Want to see the dogs?" he asked. When Donnie nodded, the man whistled, and a mother dog ran out of her kennel. She was followed by five frisky little puppies and one more puppy that lagged behind the rest.

"What's wrong with him?" asked the boy, pointing to the dog that could not keep up with the litter. The man explained that the puppy had something wrong with his hip.

"That's the very one I want," cried the boy, his eyes following each faulty movement of the puppy with growing excitement. "And I know my father will let me have this dog." The man shook his head.

"No, son," he suggested. "Why don't you think about one of these frisky pups? That dog will never be able to run as you'd want him to do."

"I don't run so well myself," Donnie explained as he pulled up his trousers and pointed to a heavy brace on one of his legs. "This dog needs somebody that understands him. He's the special one I've been waiting for."

SUMMER STORM

The rounded thunderhead billowed up in the southwest. Rachel watched it and shivered when she saw a far-off flash of lightning and heard the low rumble of thunder. She was alone and terrified.

Rachel knew her older sisters and maybe her mother too would be nervous if they were home. But even a half-fearful family would be some comfort, she thought. She did not expect any of them back for several hours and wished again that she had gone with them. Why had she stayed home just to finish reading a book?

Most of all, Rachel thought of her father as she anxiously watched the fast-moving black clouds. She had often wondered why he always sat on the front porch during a summer storm. Several times he had invited her or others in the family to join him and had seemed to want company. But she had always been too frightened to go outside, and she guessed her sisters and mother must have been too.

A gusty wind began to bend the trees. She jumped as a window in an upstairs room banged shut. The first big drops of rain splashed down just as Father pulled his car into the driveway, jumped out, and ran into the house.

Rachel's heart turned over with a suffocating love for him as he explained, "Thought I'd better check on you. How about a ringside seat for an A-No.-1 attraction tonight?"

She followed him out onto the porch as Father pulled two chairs close together and then reached out a hand to take one of her trembling ones and hold it tight.

"How beautiful this all is," he said softly. "Nature's fireworks. You know, being frightened won't ever stop a storm, but facing the beauty and majestic power of it can bring a strange and exciting kind of joy—and a deep gratitude for being a part of such a wondrous world. How much people miss in life if they spend their time being afraid!"

At his quiet words, Rachel looked up and let her eyes sweep across the sky as one streak of lightning followed another while amost constant thunder growled and crashed around them. In all of her ten years she had never really seen a summer storm before. It was beautiful, she thought.

At that moment, with her father's hand tightly holding hers, Rachel decided that the rest of her life she would be glad for the beauty of the world and that she would try to have courage, even in a storm.

TURNIPS FOR THANKSGIVING

An unusually beautiful spring held a promise of plenty. Seeds were carefully planted by the Green family. Just as they began to sprout, a heavy rain came in torrents. Afterward not a seedling could be found anywhere.

Again the planting was done, but during the rainy summer there was little growth. In September it seemed as if the sky opened. Hail beat the crops into the ground. Even the potatoes rotted in mud. Only a small patch of turnips could be harvested.

"Let's just forget Thanksgiving this year," said the children. "Who could make a feast out of turnips?"

Father was thoughtful. Early on the morning of Thanksgiving he took his gun and slipped away from the house before anyone else was awake. He came back before noon with a scrawny jack rabbit for mother to cook.

That night as the family gathered for dinner, Gordon cried, "I don't want anything. That rabbit looks like a piece of old dead horse, and I hate turnips!"

Father looked at one child and then another. Finally he smiled at Mother and excused himself. The children heard him go upstairs to the attic.

The family sat around the table in miserable silence until Father came back into the room carrying an old oil lamp. He lighted it and set it in the middle of the table.

"Now, Gordon," he said, "turn out all the lights. Perhaps then in the dark we can see." He bowed his head and gave thanks for the food and for all their wonderful blessings.

When he finished, everyone was quiet. The children looked at each other in the dimly lit room.

The lamp sputtered as Gordon began to eat. Suddenly it seemed as if the jack rabbit tasted like turkey. And even the turnips were delicious!

MOTHER'S PROMISE

"Mai-mai," Elizabeth called to the old woman. She had learned this greeting from her mother. Sometimes it had seemed to Elizabeth that it would have been much easier to just pay no attention when the Indians came and stood around watching the family as they worked or played, but Mother insisted that they always be welcomed.

The one who came most often was an old woman who frequently walked to their home from her village of Temuco. Elizabeth and her family lived in Chile and spoke Spanish, but the old woman knew only the language of her people, Arauncanian Indian. Elizabeth had once complained that it was impossible to carry on a conversation and she could not understand why the old woman bothered them.

"Some time," Mother promised, "you'll know why she comes, and you'll be glad if you've made her welcome and shown her any kindness."

One day the Indian woman brought with her a few partridge eggs and a handful of berries. Each simple gift was shyly held out for approval. When Elizabeth smiled her thanks, the old woman's eyes sparkled with delight and even her copper bracelets

73

and coin necklaces seemed to shine with appreciation. Her many layers of hand-woven clothing had never looked as colorful.

Elizabeth suddenly realized that she was beginning to feel as if this strange person were a very good friend, and she looked forward to her visits. That day the girl invited the Indian woman to come again soon.

The old woman nodded as if she understood and started to leave. She had gone only a short distance when she turned back and muttered some singsong words as if they held a very important message. Elizabeth carefully repeated the words even though she had no idea what she was saying. She liked their sound, and during the next few days they kept going around in her head like a little tune. She tried to guess what they could mean and why they had been accompanied by such a special smile.

Elizabeth then began to think that perhaps her mother's promise was being fulfilled. She was sure of it a few weeks later when a missionary translated the message of her Indian friend.

She had said: "I shall come again, for I like myself when I'm near you!"

I EXPECT A BLESSING

Joseph and his brother eagerly dug the potatoes out of the moist ground. Food had been scarce for many months in the little Smith home, and for many days there had been nothing to eat but nettle greens, thistle, and sego roots. Now as they worked, they could almost taste the fluffy white vegetable mounds they were certain Mother would prepare for dinner. Maybe there would even be butter to go with the potatoes!

Just as the boys finished, their mother came out with the news that the best potatoes were to be loaded into a wagon so they could take them to the tithing office. The boys, who had already learned that their mother could not be talked out of doing what she felt was right, silently loaded the wagon. They carefully selected the best potatoes for tithing and saved the others for their own use.

Years later when Joseph F. Smith became the sixth president of the Church, he vividly remembered this incident in these words:

> I was a little boy at the time and drove the team. When we drove up to the steps of the tithing office, ready to unload the potatoes, one of the

clerks came over and said to my mother, "Widow Smith, it's a shame that you should have to pay tithing."

He said a number of other things, too, and then my mother turned on him and said, "William, you ought to be ashamed of yourself. Would you deny me a blessing? If I did not pay my tithing, I should expect the Lord to withhold His blessings from me. I pay my tithing not only because it is a law of God, but because I expect a blessing by doing so. By keeping this and other laws, I expect to prosper and to be able to provide for my family!"

THE BLACK POLISH SHOES

It was nearly sundown, and the boys and men of Willard had been busy since early morning clearing the road that Brigham Young's carriage would take to reach the bowery.

All day as Evan threw rocks out of the rutted road, he tried to think of something he could do about a coat and some shoes to wear at the choir program that was to be held before the banquet in the bowery.

Evan was only twelve, and every other member of the choir was many years older than he. They all called him their "Boy Alto."

Evan's family lived more than sixty miles away. He earned his board and room doing farm work. There was no one he felt he could talk to about his problem, and so as he walked to his room through the early dusk, he was deep in thought.

As Evan passed the general store, he saw a can of shoe polish in the window and suddenly decided what he could do for shoes.

After he put on his best pants that evening, he turned up the cuffs, took a can of shoe polish, and carefully painted some make-believe shoes on his feet.

77

He couldn't think of anything he could do about a coat, so he started toward the bowery in his shirt sleeves.

As he hurried along the road, he wiped away the tears which kept filling his eyes. He hoped no one would see them, but soon a choir member stopped him and asked why he was crying.

"I'm crying because I haven't any shoes, and I'm ashamed for Brigham Young to see me barefooted with all the big folks," Evan said simply.

"President Young won't think any the less of you for not having shoes," the lady assured him. "Come, Boy Alto, and sing with us."

Evan walked as far as the bowery entrance with her, but he would not go on. Just then Brigham Young and his party arrived. Evan wanted to run and hide, but as he turned to do so President Young held out a hand to stop him and asked, "Why are you running away? Why don't you go inside?"

"I—I sing in the choir," Evan stammered, "but I'm not dressed well enough to sing with them tonight." He looked down at his bare feet covered with shoe polish.

Brigham Young glanced down, and then with understanding he looked deep into Evan's eyes. "Don't feel bad," he said as he patted Evan's shoulder. "We're all friends."

More than sixty years later, after Evan Stephens had become a great musician, the Salt Lake Tabernacle Choir leader, and the composer of eighty-six LDS hymns, he often recalled this moment saying, "And ever after that I felt there was a personal acquaintance between me and the president."

I'VE BEEN EXPECTING YOU

Weeks had passed since any in the Thomas NcNeil family had enjoyed a good meal. They had been on the plains for many months, and their diet had been only milk from their faithful old cow and wild rose berries.

It was late in October of 1859, and the small party of pioneers was anxious to get to Utah before winter. While the adults planned the home they would build in the valley, the children dreamed of promised bread and meat and other satisfying food to fill their empty stomachs.

Long after dark the weary travelers ended their journey and camped for the night near Ogden. Before lying down to rest, however, they took time to kneel and express thanks for their safe arrival and plead for help in securing food the next day. All were half-sick and nearly starved.

Early the next morning Father walked to Ogden to try and find work to get enough money for a little food. Before noon several of the smaller children began to cry from hunger. Mother asked Margaret, who was then almost twelve years old, to go across the fields to a little house they could see from their camp and beg for squash from the pile heaped near the door.

As Margaret scuffed through the dry grass in her bare feet, she prayed for help.

Almost as soon as she had knocked at the door, a sweet voice called, "Come in! Come in! I've been expecting you." When Margaret entered, she smelled the fragrance of freshly baked bread and saw a kind old woman busily putting food into a large pan.

"Here, child," the woman said, "you carry this warm bread, and I'll take the rest. Something told me this morning to prepare extra food. I just knew you were coming."

LOST IN THE DESERT

A merciless sun beat down on the Scott family. What had started out as a happy vacation trip into the southern Utah desert had turned into a nightmare of heat and despair.

The family had left the main highway to explore the beauties of a deep rocky canyon. They did not know that the road they had taken led only into a wild, desolate, and treacherous area where there was no water and where the temperature often climbed to 125 degrees.

The road became more and more rough, and there was no place to turn around and go back. Sharp rocks jutted up. One of them ripped the crankcase, and oil gushed from it. Then the radiator split, and all its water spurted out onto the hot sand and disappeared.

The Scotts left their car to crouch in the shade of an overhanging rock. Mother talked quietly to the children, telling them stories and trying to calm their rising fears. Father had them all kneel and pray for strength and for the desire to endure until they could be rescued.

When the fiery sun went down and a full moon rose over the desert, each of the children obeyed instructions to carefully search the car for anything that might help them survive. Crayons and paste were salvaged to eat, mirrors were unscrewed to be used to signal any plane that might fly over, and Mother smeared the faces of all with lipstick and rouge to protect their skin from the heat. Handfuls of dirt were scooped up and rubbed on their arms.

The next day the canyon became an inferno of heat, and at sunset the family knelt again in the desert twilight while Father gave them a blessing.

Before daylight came again, Father and Mother started digging a hole with tire irons. They were too weak to do more than just scratch away a little dirt at a time, but they kept at it until all of the children were buried up to their necks to protect their bodies from the merciless sun.

Suddenly they heard a roar down the canyon, and the silver fuselage of a plane flashed in the sun. In a few hours the whole family had been flown to Moab, the nearest town.

The doctor who checked the family said, "It's amazing you are all alive! You must have worked at it pretty hard."

"Yes," answered Father thankfully. "We did work at it. But, more important, we prayed for it too!"

THE BOY ORGANIST

Joseph had pushed his way through the crowds of people who for hours had been gathering outside the gates. Now he was seated on the bench before the organ. Although he was only sixteen, he had been called by President Brigham Young to be the organist in the great Salt Lake Tabernacle.

An air of excitement was everywhere. From all over Utah the people had come by carriage, wagon, horseback, or on foot to celebrate the opening of the Tabernacle they had been building for more than four years.

As Joseph sat watching and listening while the big dome-shaped building filled with people, his thoughts went back to that evening in 1862 when he took part in a musical entertainment to celebrate his family's safe arrival in Salt Lake City after a long and difficult journey from their home in Norwich, England. He was only eleven then but had been giving concerts and accompanying his singing father since he was six years old.

Could he really remember when he had surprised his family by playing "The Ratcatcher's Daughter" when he was only four, or had he heard the story so many times that he actually seemed to remember? Joseph was not sure.

But he remembered well how he had carried his little melodeon (miniature organ) to Utah and how playing it had helped to cheer and ease those who had traveled with him across the rugged miles and helped them forget the tiring days in the magic of music each evening.

Reaching the Salt Lake Valley, they camped on the old Eighth Ward Square. That night they sang songs of praise and thanksgiving for their safe journey while Joseph again played his little melodeon.

President Young, who had gone to the Square to welcome the new arrivals, listened in amazement to Joseph's playing and finally exclaimed, "There is our organist for the great Tabernacle organ!"

And now here Joseph was on that exciting October morning in 1867 ready to begin playing for the first meeting to be held in the Salt Lake Tabernacle, the Thirty-Seventh Semiannual General Conference of The Church of Jesus Christ of Latter-day Saints. The organ was only about one-third finished and a loose garment had been thrown up around it for protection, but it was playable.

From many volunteers, 150 men and women had been chosen to be the official choir for this thrilling occasion. The singers took their places. The presiding authorities of the Church were on the stand, and President Brigham Young called the people to order. A hush came over the crowd. The men who were to hand pump the bellows of the organ began their hard work, and Joseph J. Daynes, the boy organist, placed his hands on the keys of the great organ, and the thrilling notes filled the huge Tabernacle as the choir began to sing: "Praise, praise, O praise the great I Am . . ."

THE MORNING CHORE

It was so dark that the sleepy seven-year-old boy could hardly find his way down the path to the barn. He had planned for days how he could get out of bed, dress, creep quietly down the stairs, take the milking bucket from the pantry shelf, and leave the house without waking anyone.

He had to feel his way in the dark barn to find the peg where the milking stool hung. His heart was beating faster than usual as he placed the stool by the cow and sat down on it. The cow did not even raise her head from the manger where she was munching hay, but a swish of her tail indicated she knew he was there.

The boy had seen his sister, Mary, milk the cow many times. He found it was not as easy as he thought it would be to get the cow's udder washed and then draw out the warm foamy milk from it. Before long his fingers and wrists ached. He had to stop often to rest them. He thought about going to the house to ask for help but decided against it. He was determined to finish the job alone.

The boy was so intent on milking that he did not realize how long it had taken, and he was surprised to find that daylight had come and smoke was curling up from the chimney when he finally left the barn and started for the house. As he entered the kitchen, Mother looked up from the stove where she was preparing breakfast and asked, "Why, Joseph, what have you been doing so early in the morning?"

He held up the milk bucket in answer and felt a warm rush of joy at his mother's smile of approval.

"Well," she said, "since you seem to be big enough, milking each morning will be your job." She paused and then questioned, "But why were you so anxious to milk that cow?"

Joseph lifted an earnest face to his mother as he answered, "I just want to help while Father is on his mission. Mamie (the name he called his sister) has so many other things to do, I thought if I could take care of the morning milking, she wouldn't have to worry about that!"

The long hours of work and the tired frustation Joseph Fielding Smith had felt while he taught himself how to milk a cow were forgotten as his mother put her arms around him, held him close, and said, "How pleased your father will be when I write and tell him that now there is a fine young man to take care of milking the cow while he is away."

THE TRADERS

It was spring, and the red sandy mountain around Kanab shone in the warm sunshine. The boys were glad their father had sent them on an errand to the Indian camp several miles beyond the fort. It was fun riding their ponies through the green-gray sagebrush instead of weeding the vegetable garden as they would be doing if they were at home.

As the boys rode, they were leading a horse to be traded to the Indians. They talked little, each one just enjoying the beauty of the world around them on the soft spring morning. It was good to be alive!

An old Navajo chief named Frank came out to greet them as the boys rode into camp. The day before, he had told their father that he wanted a good horse and so he had been expecting someone to come with one. Chief Frank helped the boys off their ponies, looked briefly at the horse they had brought to trade, and then waved toward some blankets a short distance away.

The colors and designs of the blankets were especially beautiful, but ten-year-old Jacob had warned his little brother, Walter, that they must act grown-up and make sure the trade they made was a good one. They shook their heads, and Jacob told the chief he would have to have more for the horse he had brought.

The old Indian hesitated only a minute and then brought out two buffalo robes and more blankets. The boys were wide-eyed with surprise at the generosity, but they said nothing. They rolled up the robes and blankets, laid them across the ponies, and rode home full of pride over their sharp trade.

Father was waiting as they came into the yard. His eyes widened in surprise as he lifted the heavy loads off the ponies and unrolled the blankets, but he said nothing.

He carefully looked at the blankets and robes, dividing them into two piles as he did so. His sons waited for him to speak, but he worked in silence. When he finished, he carefully rolled up the blankets he had put into one of the piles and told the boys they must return part of their trade.

The day seemed dark to Jacob and Walter as they rode back into the Indian camp, wondering how they could ever explain why they were there.

Chief Frank welcomed them with a warm smile. He lifted up his old arms to take the roll of blankets and then, before any explanation could be given, said, "I knew you'd come back. Your father is an honest man, and I knew he would not keep all the blankets. He takes care of us. He is a father to us also."

Suddenly the spring day seemed bright again and more beautiful than ever as the boys began to appreciate what a wise and beloved man their father, Jacob Hamblin, really was.

CARPET OF LOVE

As the two boys, nine and eleven years old, hurried toward their home, they were remembering every detail of the past week so they could tell their family.

Their Christmas holiday, which they had spent with one of their father's friends in the country, was just over. There had been snow and gifts and laughter and fun. But, best of all, there had been plenty of food to eat and the farmhouse was always warm.

Riding back from the country on the bus, the boys tried to remember back a few years earlier before Father had been sick for so long. There had been plenty of food then and their house had always been warm. Mother had laughed often as she cared for their lovely home.

Now they hardly had any furniture. They did not have one rug left in the whole house. But the boys reminded each other as they rode toward home on the bus not to mention this—and especially not to say anything about the beautiful bright carpet in the farmhouse they had just left.

The previous summer the boys had been invited to spend a few days in the country. When they returned, they had told the other children about many things, and Mother had listened with as much pleasure as anyone—that is, until they talked of the carpet in the living room and how it had made the whole farmhouse beautiful and how warm and soft it felt to their feet. That was when Mother had become quiet. When they looked at her, she hastily wiped away a tear.

"Some day," she said, "we'll have a beautiful and warm carpet too. I promise you."

The boys were almost home now. They were anxious to share their gifts, to tell about their holiday, and to be with their family again.

The elder of the two boys was first to reach their front door. He ran into the living room and then stopped suddenly, looking down in amazement. There on the floor was a beautiful turkey-red oriental carpet.

Mother hurried to greet the boys, whose eyes were wide and questioning as they looked first at her and then at the floor. Finally she said, "It's probably silly, but this is my Christmas present to us. I painted it. It won't keep your feet warm but it is pretty, don't you think?

The boys looked at her again and then at the floor, where she had painted a brilliant carpet design over the rough boards. Their eyes filled with tears. The rug was more beautiful than anything they had seen in the country, and suddenly their feet felt almost as warm as their hearts.

REMEMBERING FATHER'S COUNSEL

The little log cabin in Winter Quarters was not quite finished, but Orson Spencer and his six children moved into it anyway. They were anxious to get settled before Father left for England, where he had been called by President Brigham Young to publish a newspaper for the Church.

Father had told Ellen, who had just turned fourteen, and Aurelia, who was twelve, that they were to be "little mothers" to the four younger children. Lucy, the baby, was barely three years old. Their mother had died soon after the family left Nauvoo, so their father ferried them across the Missouri River and then hurried to build the cabin before he left.

He bought eight cows so there would be plenty of milk to drink and enough to sell. They also owned a horse that was to be sold to buy food.

Two of the girls were just recovering from an illness when late in the fall their father said goodbye to them. Friends in neighboring cabins had agreed to help the children if they were needed.

The winter was long, cold, and lonely. Many people in the little community died. Among them were several friends of the Spencer children.

Aurelia wrote in her diary:

We got through the first part of the winter pretty well, but it was uncommon in its severity. Our horse and all our cows but one died. Therefore, we had no milk or butter. Our provisions had also nearly given out so that in the spring and summer following we really suffered for something to eat. Part of the time we had nothing but cornmeal, which was stirred up with water and baked on a griddle. Many a night I went to bed without supper, having to wait until I was hungry enough to eat our poor fare.

Then one day late in the fall of 1847 President Brigham Young went to visit the Spencers' one-room log cabin. He found it neat and the children clean. Their father had been gone about a year, and the Saints had begun making preparations to start their move to the mountains in the West the following spring.

The children told President Young that their father wrote often to them, making suggestions as to what they should wear, how to comb their hair, what to do if they became ill, and how to take care of each other. They brought out the last letter they had received. After President Young read it, he told them he had a very important matter for them to think about. He asked, "What would you say if your father stayed in England at least another year? We need him there."

The children looked at each other and then waited for Ellen to speak since she was the oldest. "If it is thought best," Ellen said quietly, "we would like it so, for we want to do the best."

All the other children agreed. They remembered

that Father had once written, "Though He slay us, we should trust in Him, and all will be right."

They had faith in their father, in his counsel, and in their Father in heaven. So in the spring of 1848, the Spencer children, with determination and grateful hearts, began their preparations to move west with the Saints.

JIMMY GOES FISHING

Jimmy's mother was very ill. For more than a week she had not been able to eat even a mouthful of food. Nothing the doctor could do for her seemed to help. Only when the bishop came and he and Father blessed her, did Mother seem to be a little more comfortable.

But still she could not eat, and Jimmy was worried.

When Mother first became ill, he was disappointed because he and Dad could not go fishing even though they had their gear all ready. But now nothing mattered except Mother's getting well again, and Jimmy prayed with all his heart that she would.

"If only I could do something to help," he thought as he slowly began to take off his clothes and get ready for bed. Over in the corner stood the new fishing pole his father had brought home just before his mother took sick. It reminded him of last year when he and Dad had gone fishing and how pleased Mother was when she cooked the fish he had caught.

"I've never tasted anything so delicious in all my life," he remembered her saying.

Jimmy's heart began to beat faster at the memory. Then instead of going to bed as he had planned, he put his clothes back on and went out on the back lawn to look for night crawlers.

Just before dawn the next morning Jimmy, pole in hand, slipped out of the house and pedaled his bike to the nearby canyon. As he cast his line into the mountain stream, he closed his eyes for a moment and prayed that he might get a special fish just for Mother.

A few hours later Jimmy was back in his own driveway. Father was waiting for him, and he was worried. When he saw the fishing pole, he said tiredly, "Your mother is no better, Jimmy, and this is no time to go fishing."

Jimmy pulled a shining trout from the creel slung over his shoulder and handed it to his father. "This is for Mother," he said. "I think she can eat it."

A little later Jimmy stood in the doorway of his mother's room. Dad was sitting beside her holding a plate on which was a golden brown, sizzling hot trout. "Jimmy got this for you," he said. "I hope you can eat just a little." Then he gently lifted a forkful and put it into her mouth.

Jimmy watched while his mother carefully chewed and swallowed. For a long moment nothing happened, and then Mother turned her head to look at Jimmy standing anxiously in the doorway. She smiled weakly and nodded her head. Father, too, looked at Jimmy, and a broad smile broke over his worried face as he took another forkful of fish and put it into Mother's mouth.

THE NEW QUILT

Thanksgiving Day was cold. Gray soggy clouds covered the sun, and in the little cabin David, ten, and Eliza, eight, wished Father would come back from southern Utah with food for the winter. They hoped he would bring wool too so that Mother might make warm clothing and especially a quilt for their bed. They had had such a pretty new one early in the fall, but Mother had given it to an Indian woman who needed it to wrap her sick baby against the wind.

"It was such a pretty quilt," Eliza had said, crying a little when the Indian left.

"And such a warm one too," Mother had added. "I had counted on it for keeping you children warm all winter. But perhaps your father will bring some wool from the south so I can make another one."

Months had passed since that day. Father had not yet come home. The family had little food, and the children had to snuggle close at night to keep warm.

David had been excited when he was able to get a pheasant for Mother to roast for Thanksgiving dinner. She had used almost the last of their flour to make dumplings and the very last of the dried apples for a pie to celebrate this special day.

Mother asked an unusually long blessing on the dinner, praying for help in getting food for winter and for Father's safe return. Everything looked so good and smelled so delicious that Eliza and David could hardly wait to begin the meal.

Just as they started eating, they heard the sound of a horse and, looking out the small window, David saw the head of an Indian. Eliza was frightened and even David paled, but Mother's face brightened when she recognized the Indian woman to whom she had given the quilt.

The Indian got off her horse and tied it to the hitching post. Then she began unloading buckskin bags. She handed them to Mother. There was corn in one bag, honey in another. There was a large slab of venison and a sage hen. And, last of all, she took a beautiful warm bearskin from the horse's back and laid it on the chair inside the door.

After the Indian woman had left, taking with her the pheasant and a big piece of the dried apple pie, Mother and the children just sat and looked at each other for a few minutes. Then they bowed their heads again. There wasn't much of the dinner left on the table, but everyone agreed this was the best Thanksgiving they had ever had.

SURPRISES

It was still quite dark, but there was the soft gray-ness that comes just before dawn. Everyone in the house was asleep except Jeanie.

Almost as if an alarm clock had been set in her, she awoke each morning around five o'clock. This had started before Christmas when she would awaken early, lie for a few minutes in the warmth of her bed-clothes, and then jump out of bed and rush to see if Santa Claus had come during the night.

At first the family had been most understanding. After all, Jeanie was not yet six, and Christmas is an exciting time. But it had been nearly three months since Christmas, and Jeanie still puttered around the house before daylight every morning.

Whenever she was asked why she got up so early, her answer was always the same—she wanted to see if there were a surprise. For a while the family mem-bers accepted the answer with tolerant amusement, but finally they insisted that something be done about the early morning noises that robbed them of extra hours of sleep each day.

Jeanie could not understand why everyone was so cross about being awakened early every morning. To her it was the most exciting time of the whole day.

98

As she slipped out of bed the next morning, she tried to be so quiet that not a sound could be heard, but as she ran quickly to the big kitchen window, she stumbled and fell CRASH against a chair. Even though her arm was throbbing, she only moaned softly to herself as she sat down on the floor to rock her body to ease the momentary pain.

Mother heard the noise of the fall, of course, and hurried out of bed to see what had happened. When she was sure that Jeanie was not seriously hurt, she pulled the little girl onto her lap and told her firmly that she must stop the foolish habit of getting out of bed so early every morning to look for surprises. She explained that Christmas was over for the year and would not come again for many months.

Jeanie had been able to hold back the tears when she fell, but Mother's scolding was too much. "I'm not looking for Christmas surprises," she sobbed. "I'm looking for other surprises—like yesterday morning it was raining, and this morning the sky is clear. Maybe the sun will start making everything green by tomorrow. Oh, there's some special surprise every single morning!"

Later when Mother explained the matter to the family, everyone agreed that Jeanie should be allowed to get up as early as she wanted to look for her "surprises"—even if she did make a little noise—and that maybe some of the others in the family might join her too for a moment of discovery every new day!

THE PERFECT HIDING PLACE

Mark was lonely. It had been so good having his sister home from school on Saturday and Sunday. But now it was Monday, and Mark's sister Linda had gone to school.

As soon as his mother had finished the breakfast dishes, both she and Mark put on their sweaters and hurried across the country road where Mrs. Mills was hanging out her wash.

Marsha, the daughter of Mrs. Mills, was only five, and when she saw Mark she shouted for him to come and play. The children played happily near the clotheslines while their mothers talked. Then Marsha caught a glimpse of her friend Sandra as she came out of her home nearby. "Let's play hide 'n seek," she suggested, "and see if Sandra can find us."

Hand in hand the little friends ran across the yard and ducked into the garage. A huge old milk refrigerator stood empty in a far corner. Just a few days before, Marsha's father had taken out the cement sacks he had stored there and had not yet filled it with anything else. It seemed a perfect hiding place for the two children!

Mark and Marsha climbed inside, and as they did

so the heavy double doors slammed shut behind them. Both children began to call for help. They pounded on the doors and walls of their prison until their voices were almost gone, then they sank down crying with fright and exhaustion. Their clothes were damp from their exertion and from their struggle just to breathe in the hot airless box.

Suddenly Marsha stopped crying and said, "Don't cry, Mark. Let's pray." As Mark tried to control his sobs, Marsha began an anguished prayer.

At that moment the children's mothers, who had been frantically calling and searching the neighborhood for their little ones, decided to look in the garage "just once more." It was Marsha's voice raised in prayer, sounding faintly from a dark corner, that led to the discovery of the two children and to the saving of their lives.

A few years later Mark and several of his boyfriends decided to see if, standing just outside the garage, they could hear one of them loudly call from within the huge refrigerator. Repeated experiments made them all agree that it would have been impossible to have heard the voices of Marsha and Mark unless their mothers' hearing had been "quickened" at the moment of great need.

AN ENEMY PARTY

It was recess time. Pat and Peggy sat on the school steps watching the boys and girls playing together. They were never invited to join the others. They were glad they were twins so they did not have to be all alone in the new school, but each one knew how lonely the other was.

It seemed as if it were impossible for them to make any friends. Often their talk was of the fun they had had at school before they had moved into a strange big city because of Father's work.

Pat and Peggy agreed that the most popular girl in the school was a beautiful blonde named Lola. They were sure that if they could make friends with her, the other girls and boys would neither avoid them nor tease them as they did. But every day Lola seemed to think up a different way to torment the sisters and keep the other children from becoming friendly.

After dinner that night Father put down his evening paper, looked at the two girls, who sat glumly across the room not even interested in a television program, and shook his head. He turned back as if to read his paper, but instead he sat with his head bowed in deep thought.

Finally he smiled to himself, looked up at Pat and Peggy, and invited them to come sit on the arms of his chair. "Now tell me," he said, "just what is wrong with my usually happy duo?"

The twins looked at each other but did not answer.

In a minute Father asked some other questions: "Is something wrong at school? Is it too hard for you? Are you sorry we moved?"

At first no response came, but finally Peggy and Pat began to tell him of their loneliness. Once the girls started talking, it seemed they could not stop. The whole story of their unfriendly treatment at school tumbled out into his sympathetic ears.

When they were finally through, Father said, "I know what we'll do. Let's have a party."

At first Pat and Peggy were delighted. They began talking excitedly about ice cream and cake and balloons, but then they stopped. "Who can we invite to a party?" they cried. "We haven't any friends." Then their tears started again.

Father's eyes twinkled as he answered, "Oh, we won't worry about inviting friends right now. We'll have an enemy party. We'll just invite all those unfriendly boys and girls in your class at school and see what happens."

And that is exactly what Pat and Peggy McEvoy did. Almost every one came who was invited, and when they left they all declared it was the best party they had ever attended.

Even though everyone had a wonderful time, Pat and Peggy never had another enemy party. They no longer knew anyone to invite because they suddenly had only friends at the new school—especially Lola!

THE GOLD STAR

"You are each to write a poem for Mother's Day," the teacher said. The girls in the third-grade class smiled at each other and quickly started writing. But the boys looked uncomfortable and wondered what they could write, especially Roberto.

The teacher told them that the one who wrote the best poem about mother would have a gold star pasted by his or her name on the blackboard. Roberto half-closed his eyes, trying to imagine what it would be like to see his name with a big shining gold star beside it. But his dream lasted only a moment, for he was sure that no poem he wrote would ever be judged as the best one.

Roberto looked at the blank sheet his teacher had given him. He bounced his pencil on its eraser end and then started to make some marks on the paper.

"I could easily draw a star," he decided, "lots of them, but that wouldn't mean very much, not nearly as much as if a big gold one were placed beside my name on the blackboard!"

Debbie waved her hand. "I'm through," she announced when the teacher called on her. "May I read my poem now?"

104

"All the poems will be read at three o'clock, and you may read yours first," the teacher promised.

Promptly at three, the teacher called on Debbie, who stood up proudly and read:

Mothers buy dresses and shoes and things.
They give us parties and rings.
We wish them a happy Mother's Day.
We hope mothers are here to stay.

Bobby was next:

Mothers make clown suits and lemonades
And fix sore toes with keen Band-aids;
But there's one thing she can't do, and I wish
    she could—
That's learn to like bugs, like mothers should.

Eagerly the children read the poems they had written for their mothers, all except Roberto.

"I can't make a poem," he explained when it was his turn. "The words don't rhyme."

The children exchanged amused smiles.

"But I've written what I feel," he continued. Then Roberto read:

Mothers . . . mothers make . . .
Well, mothers make you hurt inside
When you haven't got one.

He looked around at the boys and girls, expecting them to laugh because he could not write a poem, but there was no laughter from them.

And everyone in the third grade was glad when their teacher put a big gold star on the blackboard next to the name of Roberto José Martinez.

THE FEEDBOX

The sun was especially hot in St. George, Utah. Not the faintest breeze stirred the heavy air.

Seven-year-old Lealand and eight-year-old John had been playing in the shade all morning. But it was hot even in the shade, and the boys were hungry as the sun climbed toward the high point in the sky that would tell them it was noon and that their mothers would soon have lunch ready.

While they waited, they decided to rest on a large box Lealand's father had placed just outside the corral. After a while the boys lifted the heavy tin-lined lid to see inside, and they were fascinated with the crickets hopping around in the bottom of the box where only a handful of feed was left.

What fun it would be to catch the crickets, they thought! Taking off their shoes, they placed them on the ground by the box and then helped each other into it.

The box had been carefully lined with tin to keep out storm and moisture and was barely large enough for them to squeeze inside. So the boys quickly decided that it was too uncomfortable to stay inside. But before they could climb back out, a cow that was eating in the manger nearby tossed her head and flipped the lid back over the box. The strong lock caught, and Lealand and John were held prisoners inside the nearly airtight box.

Lealand and John called for help with all their strength, but no one heard their muffled cries.

Only a threadlike crack where the lid fit over the top let in any of the hot air. In their cramped positions, the boys tried to keep their noses as near this crack as possible. But every minute the box became hotter and the oxygen became less.

The boys could hardly breathe when John said, "Oh, Lealand, let's pray. No one else can hear us, but Heavenly Father can." So the boys whispered a fervent prayer.

Almost at once the boys heard Lealand's little brother, Wesley, outside. He was pulling his wagon around the yard and stopped when he noticed two pairs of shoes near the big box. Although he was only four years old, he quickly opened the lock.

Lealand and John were almost too weak to push up the heavy lid when the lock was undone. Wet with perspiration, they gulped big breaths of fresh air until they had enough strength to climb out of the box and stagger gratefully into the house.

THE BASEBALL PLAYER

Heber's arm ached, but he kept throwing the ball against the old adobe barn. He was tall and lean and not very strong, but he was determined to be a good baseball player. As he threw the ball, he thought how glad he was to have a ball of his very own, and he vowed to make good use of it every possible minute.

There were three baseball teams in his neighborhood. He was on the third team with the youngest and the poorest players. All of the other boys Heber's age were on the first team, and they teased him about playing with the "little kids."

His mother was a widow. His father died when Heber was only nine days old. He and his mother lived in a small house where she took in sewing and prepared food for boarders.

Heber knew that if he were ever going to be a good baseball player, he would need to practice. But he didn't have a ball, and his mother had no money to buy him one.

He had thought and prayed about the matter. Then one day some of this mother's boarders offered to pay Heber to keep their boots shined.

It took a long time for Heber to shine enough

boots to earn the money to buy a ball, but finally one joyful day he was able to take one home to show his mother. She knew how anxious he was to be a good player, and so she secured permission for him to practice by throwing the ball against the neighbor's adobe barn.

Bishop Woolley often stopped to watch Heber as he threw and caught the ball until it sometimes seemed that the barn gable would be pounded in. At first the would-be baseball player was so awkward that Bishop Woolley would just shake his head as he watched him and then murmur something about "such a waste of time" as he walked away.

Weeks and then months went by. Every free minute Heber practiced throwing and catching the ball. Heber's arm ached so that he could hardly sleep nights, and it pained him when he used it during the day.

Before the summer was over, he made the second team. Then finally one day he was asked to play on the first team with the boys his own age.

When Heber grew to be a young man, he was on the Red Stocking baseball team that played for the championship of the entire Utah Territory.

All of his boyish heartaches over baseball and all of the hours of practice through the years were forgotten at the moment the Red Stockings were crowned the territory baseball champions. At that time Heber J. Grant was credited with being one of the team's best players.

THE SHOEMAKER OF TRONDHEIM

John and his two-year-old brother lived with their mother in Trondheim, Norway. After Father's death they had moved from Froya to a small apartment on Steensbakken (Steen's Hill). The two little boys and their mother often looked out over the beautiful old city on the outermost island off the coast of Norway. They could also see how the harbor and the fjord zigzagged toward the ocean.

Running up and down the hill helped to wear out John's shoes. One day his mother asked a neighbor to recommend someone to repair them.

The neighbor, a ship's captain, said he knew just the right person to suggest. "In fact," the captain said, "the shoemaker's son will soon deliver some shoes to me, and then he can take back those of John's that need repairing."

A few days later the boy brought back John's shoes neatly mended. A strange little pamphlet was inside each one.

Some time later John's mother wrapped another pair of shoes into a package, tucked it under her arm, and set out on the half-hour walk to the shoemaker's shop. When she returned, she was restless. She had a rather strange look and seemed to be unusually quiet and thoughtful.

When the shoemaker's son delivered the second pair of shoes, new pamphlets were carefully tucked into each shoe. The next Sunday John's mother arranged for someone to be with the boys while she went to a meeting at the shoemaker's sturdy log house.

It was not until some years later that she told John what the shoemaker had said when she went to his shop with the second pair of shoes to be repaired and to ask him about the pamphlets he had put in the shoes. They were words she could never forget.

"You may be surprised," he answered, "to hear me say that I can give you something of more value than soles for your child's shoes. I can teach you, as you have never known it before, the love of God for his children on earth."

The pamphlets were missionary tracts of The Church of Jesus Christ of Latter-day Saints. Because of them John, his mother, and his brother became members of the Church. Forty-two years later John A. Widtsoe, who was then president of the University of Utah, was called to be a member of the Quorum of the Twelve Apostles.

Just as he had promised, the shoemaker in Trondheim, Norway, did give to John A. Widtsoe's mother and her family something of far more value than soles for a worn pair of shoes.

THE STANDBY PITCHER

David had been playing for a little league team all season. More than anything else, he wanted to be a regular on the team, and he wanted to be a pitcher.

He never missed a practice or a game. Whenever his dad or his older brother could find the time, he would get them to play catch with him. Even when David watched television, he would wear his baseball mitt and pop a ball in and out of it almost automatically. Sometimes he would forget to take the mitt off when his mother called him for meals, and then the family would have to wait while David put the mitt away, washed his hands, and came to the table.

Near the end of the season the coach told all the little leaguers they should meet at the ball park on a certain Sunday morning to have a special practice and to have their pictures taken.

"I can't come on Sunday," said David.

"You'd better," said the coach, "because we're going to talk about our team for next year after we have our pictures taken."

Usually David ran home full of excitement after a ball game or a practice. But this night he was late, and he hardly answered when his family spoke to him.

He was unusually quiet all week, but on Sunday he did not go to the ball park. On Monday he was at practice and at every practice afterward.

Finally the day came for the team tryouts. "You'll be one of our regular pitchers," the coach told David, "but you'll have to play whenever a game is scheduled. We need you—and that will mean sometimes you will play on a Sunday."

"I'm sorry, but I can't play ball on Sunday," David said.

"Then you'll have to be a standby pitcher instead of a regular one," answered the coach.

And that was how the season went. Sometimes David had a chance to pitch a game, but more often he did not. The other boys on the team played on Sunday, but David went to Sunday School and sacrament meeting with his family.

In the spring when David was ten years old, the coach called the boys together to begin a new season and to make selections for the team. "We'll need you for a regular pitcher this year, David," he said. "But sometimes you'll need to play on Sunday."

"I'll have to think about it," said David.

That night he talked the problem over with his dad and then said a special prayer to help him have the courage to do what he knew was right.

The next day he told the coach he would have to be just a standby pitcher again. The coach only shook his head.

Several weeks went by, and David was at every practice. One night the coach called the boys around him. He explained that David could not play ball on Sunday even though the team often had a game on that day. "But I'd like him to be our pitcher anyhow," he went on. "If you agree, we could let David be our regular weekday pitcher and have a standby pitcher for Sunday games. How about it?"

There was a moment of silence. David could hardly breathe. The team members hesitated for only a minute, and then every little leaguer agreed wholeheartedly to the Sunday standby pitcher plan.

SARAH'S DOLL

The only doll Sarah ever had was the little wooden one her brother Jim carved from a pine limb. Mother painted on a face and then wrapped the limb in some old dresses so it was soft and cuddly for Sarah.

She loved this doll more than anything in the world—except her mother and father and Jim, of course. It was the only thing of her very own she had been able to take with her to the Big Muddy when Father was called to leave their comfortable log cabin and go out to begin a new settlement. She took the doll to bed with her every night.

Mother knows how much I love my doll, Sarah thought, so she doesn't really want me to give it away. She hugged the doll close.

But again Sarah heard her mother's words, "The little papoose wants your doll, dear. Will you give it to her? Father would want you to be friends. You must be a brave little pioneer."

Sarah had heard her father say many times they should think kindly of the Indians who lived near them and they should all be friends. She remembered he had given the Indians many things the family had needed for themselves.

She looked up, silently pleading to keep her doll,

but Mother only smiled tenderly and nodded. Sarah hesitated a moment longer and then held out her beloved doll to the Indian child who kept pointing toward it.

Then Sarah turned to run toward the wagon that was now their home. Her eyes were so blinded with tears that she stumbled and fell, crushing her nose against a jagged rock. The blood gushed out in red streaks onto the dusty ground. Sarah was too numb and hurt to cry.

Mother tried to stop the flow of blood by bathing Sarah's face and nose in cold water from the nearby stream, but it was soon clear that this was no ordinary nosebleed.

Father and Jim were hunting, but Sarah's mother knew she must have help. There was no one near except the Indian women who had come to the wagon with the little papoose to ask for the doll. They had now started back to their own camp, but quickly Mother ran after them.

The women hurried back, gathered small smooth pebbles from the cold brook, and covered Sarah's neck and head with them. Whenever the stones began to warm, they were changed for cold ones. It was not long until the bleeding lessened and finally stopped.

Sarah was chilled from the cold pebble packs the women had used and weak from the loss of so much blood. Carefully they helped Mother carry her into the wagon and place her on her own bed to rest.

As Sarah turned to say goodbye to these friends who had helped save her life, the mother of the little Indian girl took the wooden doll from her daughter's arms and gently placed it next to Sarah murmuring, "Good papoose! Brave little pale face."

Sarah lovingly hugged her doll, smiled her thanks, and was soon asleep.

THE WATER PARADE

Inside the log fort called Bryan's Station, the thirsty children asked again and again for something to drink. Worried mothers comforted them but could give them no water. Anxious fathers kept a constant watch as the white renegade, Simon Girty, led more than a thousand Indian warriors into the woods surrounding the fort. They moved silently, hoping for a surprise attack the next day.

Girty had made a careful count of the Kentucky settlers in the fort. He knew they were hopelessly outnumbered against his forces, for there were only fifty men with fifty rifles. And no water. Without it, the station could not possibly be held until reinforcements arrived from Lexington.

Throughout the long night the children slept little and stirred often, moaning in their sleep. The grown-ups did not sleep at all. The only sound to be heard outside was the noise made by a spring that flowed by the woods where Girty's warriors were gathering.

It was the custom for the women of Bryan's Station to take their buckets each morning and cross the clearing to get water. They had not dared to do so the previous day, and now all the buckets were empty. If the men were to go, they might be killed instantly, but without water the whole group would surely die.

As dawn began to lighten the sky, those within the fort knelt for morning prayer to ask for inspiration to know what to do. It was decided to send the children for water. The belief was that Girty would not harm any of them since to do so would spoil his surprise attack.

The children dressed and were given the empty buckets. They were told to walk very slowly, to act as if they did not know the woods were full of warriors, and to pretend they were not frightened.

Led by a few women, the children waited as the gates of the fort were opened. Then in the early summer morning they crossed the clearing to the spring. They filled the buckets, looking about as if they thought of nothing but the beauty of a new day.

Breathlessly their parents watched from every peephole in the fort. Each minute seemed an eternity.

The children slowly walked back across the clearing with their precious supply of water. Several of them lingered to pick flowers, and one child stopped to carefully examine a rock in his path. At last they reached the fort. The heavy gates, which would hold until help arrived, were closed behind them.

The children set down their buckets and ran to loving fathers and mothers who clasped them close.

EARLY HALLOWEEN

For weeks Betsy had watched the pumpkin patch turn from golden yellow to bright orange. She had picked out the prettiest one of all for her very own, and Father had said she could have it for Halloween.

Then early one morning he woke her to say that Mother's arm was much worse and that he would have to take her into the neighboring settlement to the doctor. Ten-year-old Betsy wondered how she could ever take care of the chores and her younger brother and sister all day. But when she saw the worried look on Father's face, she did not mention her concern.

Just as the wagon pulled away from the house, Father suggested that the children might pick some pumpkins and stack them at the back of the house.

"Even mine?" asked Betsy.

"Even yours," he answered as they rode away.

Mother and Father had not come home by the time the sun went down. As long as there was daylight, the children watched the clearing for Father's wagon. But soon an uneasy darkness forced them inside.

So that the others would not worry, Betsy involved

all of them in making Halloween jack-o-lanterns. She lit the candle on the table and gave the children spoons to scoop out the seeds and pulp from the pumpkins before carving faces.

She had just finished her own special pumpkin when the pounding of horses' hooves was heard.

The children looked up expectantly. "Mother?" they asked.

Betsy shook her head and then hurried each child under the bed. "Indians," she whispered to herself.

The quiet of the evening was soon broken by the shouts of the Indians who surrounded the little house. Betsy's thoughts were in a turmoil as she breathed a prayer for help.

"What shall I do? Oh, what shall I do?" she murmured, and then the thought came to her to place the lighted candle in her pumpkin. She took the pumpkin in both hands and, standing on her tiptoes, held the grinning jack-o-lantern up to the window.

Almost immediately the Indians slowed their horses, held an excited discussion, and then turned and rode away.

It was late when Father and Mother arrived home to hear the story from the still frightened and sleepy children.

"Those Indians must have thought there were evil spirits living here," chuckled Father. "I'm proud of your quick thinking. How brave you are."

THE PROMISE

Joseph sat on a stone near a gate beyond which he could see a large house. Every once in a while he brushed away a tear that ran down his cheek.

When his father had died several years before, his mother had not been able to take care of the children, so she had arranged for them to live with various relatives. Joseph had been sent to Islip to live with a married brother. The brother, William, had not been pleased, but at least he provided food to eat and a cot on which the boy could sleep.

But now Joseph had no home, no food, no money, and no idea where to go or what to do. He did not even know how to find the two missionaries who had been the cause of all his troubles. Yet somehow he was still glad he had met them. How it had thrilled him when they had promised that the Lord hears and answers the prayers of those who seek help. Joseph had really sought!

He remembered how excited he had been that first night he had talked with the missionaries and how he had hurried home to tell his brother about them. But William would not listen. In fact, he warned the boy that if he were friendly with them, Joseph could no longer live in his home.

At first Joseph avoided the missionaries, but something about them had made him go again to hear them speak. Early this morning he tried to make William understand why, but the older brother, furious at being disobeyed, ordered the boy out of his house and told him never to come back.

Joseph did not know how far he had walked before he sat down on the rock to rest. He had not been there long when a carriage come down the road from the house and stopped at the gate.

Without thinking, Joseph jumped up and hurried to open it. The man in the carriage was pleased at the boy's eagerness to help. Seeing his smudged and tear-streaked face, he invited Joseph to go back up the road with him for something to eat.

Afterward the man and his wife listened quietly while Joseph told them about his brother. Then the childless couple invited Joseph to work for and to stay with them. They promised too that they would help him find the Mormon missionaries, and Joseph knew that they would.

In a shining moment of relief, Joseph breathed a prayer of thankfulness for his new-found friends—the man and woman who were to become like parents to him, and the missionaries whose promise had surely been fulfilled.

The year was 1842. The place was England. Joseph Robinson was eleven.

FROM DARK TO LIGHT

Gray shadows of disappointment nagged at Karl as he walked home in the dark between the two elders who had just baptized and then confirmed him a member of the Church. He had prayed that he might know whether the Church had been dreamed up by man or whether it had truly been established by the Lord, and he had fully expected the horizon to lighten when he came up out of the Elbe River.

But the night was still dark and the sky was still black. No sign had been given.

As the three returned home through the dark together, their discussion centered on the authority of the priesthood. One of the elders spoke German and interpreted for Karl, who spoke only German, and then interpreted for the other elder, who spoke only English. Then miraculously and suddenly there was no need for an interpreter. For a short time both elders understood Karl's questions and comments, and Karl understood their answers whether spoken in German or English!

Karl knew that his prayer at the time of his baptism had been answered, and the elders also knew this strange experience was a special blessing for all of them. What they did not know then was that Karl's baptism would prove to be a great blessing to all of the Church.

Dr. Karl G. Maeser was twenty-seven at the time of his baptism and held the position of *oberlehrer* (head teacher) at the Budig Academy in Dresden. A brilliant student and teacher, he had first learned of the Mormon Church through a popular pamphlet written to ridicule its teachings. He wondered what could cause anyone to have such hatred for a church, and he decided to learn more about it.

There were no Mormons in the country around Dresden at that time, but Karl accidentally discovered there were missionaries in Denmark. So he wrote to the mission president there for information and was sent pamphlets and books. Carefully studying the material, he became interested in the teachings of the Church and asked that a missionary be sent to Dresden to explain things to him. Two months later, in October 1855, Karl became the first member of the Church in that area of Germany.

Twenty-one years later, in the spring of 1876, Dr. Maeser, who had immigrated to the United States, was teaching school in the Twentieth Ward schoolhouse in Salt Lake City when a blast destroyed the building. Reporting the explosion to President Brigham Young, Karl said the school would have to be closed.

"That is exactly right, Brother Maeser," President Young replied, "For I have another mission for you." And that is how Karl G. Maeser was told of his call to establish the Brigham Young University in Provo, Utah.

On the dark night of his baptism, Karl had no way of knowing that his love for people and the gospel would brighten the horizons of all those whose lives he touched.

Grandchildren and great-grandchildren of his students still quote many of the sayings of this great teacher. Some of his most famous are these: "Whatever you do, don't do nothing," and "Be yourself, but always your better self."

SUMMER RAIN

Nell was so excited she could hardly wait to change her Sunday clothes and run out to tell Papa what she had learned at conference. She did not even take time to put on her shoes but ran barefoot across the dusty yard.

It was June 1899. There had been no rain in southern Utah for more than two years. The streams and even the wells around St. George had dried up. No crops could grow without water, and thousands of cattle had died on the range.

Some of the families had already moved, and now Papa was also preparing to leave. Earlier that morning he had decided he was too busy packing the wagon to go to conference, even though President Lorenzo Snow had come all the way from Salt Lake City to talk to the people.

"Papa! Oh, Papa!" Nell called as she ran to him. "You can take our things out of the wagon. We don't have to leave! In conference today President Snow said that if the people will pay their tithing and plant their fields, the rains will come and we'll have food."

But Papa did not seem to understand. He just

shook his head and sat down on the tongue of the wagon staring out across the barren fields.

Papa had explained again and again that they could not live through another year without rain. There was very little food on their pantry shelves, and all the money that was left was the twenty dollars that Grandfather had given to Nell before he died.

Later that evening as Papa was washing up for dinner, Nell overhead him tell her mother that they should all be ready to start at six the next morning. "We can make Thomson's ranch by noon if we do," he said.

As the family sat down to a simple meal, no one spoke. Nell felt so sad she could hardly choke down the food. Finally she swallowed hard and said, "Grandfather once told me a story about how the people were blessed by doing exactly as Brigham Young asked them to do."

Her father and mother stopped eating to listen as Nell continued, "When I said I wished I had lived then so I could have followed a prophet, Grandfather said that President Snow is our prophet today just like Brigham Young was then and that we should all follow him."

After Nell finished telling the story, she asked Papa to take her precious twenty dollars. "You can give it to Bishop Thorne," she explained, "to help bring rain to St. George!"

Early the next morning Nell looked out the window and saw a great cloud of dust blowing at the far end of the field. Her father had just started plowing their land. She dressed quickly and ran out across the dry ground.

When Papa saw her, he stopped the horses and held out his arms. Nell flew into them, and he held her close. "Good morning, sleepyhead," he said. "I thought you'd never get here in time to help me plow the field and plant our seeds!"

During the hot dry weeks that followed, the people of St. George anxiously scanned the cloudless sky and sadly shook their heads. But neither Nell nor her father were surprised when on the second day of August it began to rain!

A PIONEER BOY

The cold November wind rattled the door so hard that John was afraid his feeble knock might not be heard. His two-year-old sister strapped to his back stirred restlessly, but the five-month-old baby he carried in his arms, wrapped in a wolfskin, lay so still that John was afraid she might be dead. Four other children—a younger brother and three sisters—huddled close to him.

The weary group led by the thirteen-year-old boy had come more than five hundred miles over the Oregon Trail. They had started out in June with a large pioneer company. But when John's father and mother had become ill, they had been forced to drop behind the company to rest.

After his parents died in July, John abandoned the old wagon. Then the oxen died. The heat was scorching in the daytime, and the cold was miserable at night. Across the barren plains and over the mountains the little pioneers crept west.

When they reached Fort Boise, John was almost naked. He wore only ragged buckskin pants and even more ragged moccasins. The government agent there gave the children food and offered to keep the baby and the two smallest sisters, but John insisted that the family stay together. The agent gave the boy a horse and sent two Indians along to help him. After a few days' travel, the Indians left the party, taking the horse with them.

Now the children were alone again except for their old cow, which John kept because she provided a little milk for the baby.

It was late fall now, and snow lay deep in the mountain passes. In crossing a river the oldest girl fell and broke her leg. John packed the broken leg with snow to keep the swelling down and lifted the girl onto the cow's back. The children staggered on.

At last they reached the top of the last mountain and wound their way down to the little mission home in the beautiful Columbia Valley below.

John knocked at the mission door. It was opened by Dr. Whitman. The ragged, near-starved children hardly looked human. The doctor gasped when he lifted the wolfskin and saw the nearly lifeless form.

The children were promptly taken to a nearby shed where they were bathed and fed. John stayed to see what Mrs. Whitman could do for the baby. She rubbed the baby with warm oil and then placed a drop of hot milk between the baby's blue lips. The baby stirred, and a small squeak came from her throat.

At the sound, John dropped to his knees in a prayer of thanksgiving and then limped from the room to join the other children.

THE KEY

Christian fingered the key in his pocket as he walked toward the jail. It had taken months of study and prayer before he had finally decided to use the key for something more important than just opening the jail door so he could carry meals to those who were held prisoners.

Almost all the men in the jailhouse were Mormon missionaries. Many of them had sailed into the Port of Frederikstad in a pilot boat they had fitted up and named *Sions Löve* (Zion's Lion) so that they could easily travel to coastal areas of the Scandinavian Mission, then including all of Norway, Sweden, and Denmark.

At first Christian hadn't paid much attention to the missionaries, for he was busy learning the catechism so he could correctly answer any questions he might be asked by the priest at the confirmation service soon to be held for prospective young members of the Lutheran Church. He was not concerned about the fact that almost as soon as any Mormon missionaries arrived in Frederikstad, they were arrested.

Lutheranism was the national religion of Norway, and missionaries who taught other doctrines were promptly jailed—some for only a few weeks, others for many months. During this time they frequently were taken to court, where attempts were made to persuade them to renounce their religion and declare allegiance to the national church of Norway. Refusing to do so, they were returned to jail.

Christian worked for the warden of the jail, who instructed him to heckle and be as unpleasant as possible to the prisoners when he carried meals to them. This seemed like fun until one day a young missionary said, "Why do you talk and act as you do? Remember that so persecuted they the Christ and his followers in Bible times."

The startled boy asked him to explain what he meant, so two of the elders began talking about the gospel and gave him a copy of the Book of Mormon.

Every night as Christian studied for his confirmation examination, he also studied the Book of Mormon, comparing it with his Bible and the Lutheran catechism. As the truthfulness of the restored gospel became more and more apparent to him, Christian prayed to know what he should do. Since no answer came before the confirmation date, he purposely failed the examination and then made application to take it again in six months.

Thinking back over his months of prayer and study, Christian knew what he must do. He finally decided to use his key to the prison to let the two missionaries out of jail long enough to go with him to a nearby fjord so he could be baptized and confirmed a member of The Church of Jesus Christ of Latter-day Saints. Afterward the three walked back to the jailhouse, where the elders returned to their room and Christian turned the key in the lock to their cell.

Because of the persecution of members of the

Church throughout Norway, and also because he knew how angry his father would be, Christian did not tell anyone of the thrilling event that had taken place on that cold winter night of 1852. He knew he would not be able to make his stern father understand what he had done. He tried to talk with his mother, but she would not listen.

When the next confirmation service was held, Christian honored his application and appeared for his examination.

"Do you believe in God?" was the first question asked by the priest.

"Oh, yes," Christian answered quickly.

"Can you describe him?" was the next question.

"I know he is a Being with body, parts, and passions," Christian replied. "I also know he does not sit on the top of a topless throne. I know our Heavenly Father is good and kind—that he sees, hears, and answers prayers. I know we are made in his image as was his Son Jesus Christ."

The priest was surprised by this description but continued with the examination, becoming more and more amazed with the answers Christian gave.

As the boy glanced at his father, he could see that he was very upset.

Finally the priest said angrily, "You answer as if you belonged to that sect known as Mormons."

"I do," Christian said, "and I'm proud of it!"

At this declaration, Christian's father arose from his seat near the front of the church and rushed up the aisle and out the door, striking his cane hard against the floor with every step he took.

Confused and embarrassed, Christian's mother followed her husband, and their son was abruptly dismissed.

Christian went home wanting to talk with his

parents, but he was afraid of what they would say. Having carried his usual armful of wood into the house that night, Christian was piling it near the fireplace when his father came into the room.

At the sight of his son, who he felt had disgraced him, Christian's father struck him with his cane and then began to beat him. At last, panting for breath, his father laid the merciless cane on the table.

"Oh, Father," Christian said quietly, "it feels good to be whipped for the gospel's sake."

At these words, his father became even more furious. He picked up stick after stick of firewood and hurled them at Christian. When the wood was gone, he opened the door and shouted, "Get out of my house. I never want to see you again!"

Bruised and bleeding from the beating and the wood that had been thrown at him, Christian dragged himself out to the barn, where he threw himself upon the hay.

Late that night after her husband was asleep, Christian's mother noiselessly tied a little food and a few of his belongings in a handkerchief and went out to the barn. Tearfully she treated her son's injuries as well as she could.

"Why, oh, why did you do this thing, Christian?" she pleaded broken-heartedly.

"Because I had to, Mother," Christian replied. "I have studied and prayed, and I know this is the true Church. I tried to tell you, but you wouldn't listen to me. I cannot deny what I know, Mother. If I did, it would be to deny Jesus Christ, our Savior, and I cannot do that."

"If, as you say, you know this is right, my boy," his mother told him, "then you must stand firm. But, oh, how my heart aches."

When the first streaks of dawn appeared in the

sky, Christian's mother crept back into the house. Christian picked up the little bundle she had brought to him and started walking down the road. As he passed his house, he breathed a silent good-bye to his parents, for he knew he would never see them again.

Christian Hans Monson did not know where he would go or what he could do. "But I have a testimony," the fourteen-year-old boy said to himself. "Whatever happens, I can never deny that. And I know that because of my testimony all will be well!"

SONG OF THE PIONEERS

Four young men sat in an Indian hogan wondering why the old chief had insisted that they come to his home. Earlier that evening, as Mormon missionaries, they had held a meeting on a street corner in a little Oklahoma Indian village. They had just started to sing "Come, Come, Ye Saints" when the chief, bent and wrinkled with age, pushed his way through the crowd and quietly listened a few feet away from them. All through the meeting he stood and watched them carefully. After the closing prayer was offered, they were greatly surprised when he invited them to go to his hogan.

Now they sat quietly inside waiting to learn why they had been invited. The old chief finally began to tell them a story. He said he remembered when the Mormon pioneers were fleeing from the persecution they were forced to endure in the eastern part of the United States. He understood why they sought a place of peace in the West where they could settle. His people were angry at all white men at that time because of their mistreatment and decided to kill every one whom they met.

Then the Mormon pioneers, led by Brigham

Young, came. They had almost reached the Rocky Mountains when they stopped one evening in a little valley before attempting to go through a high mountain pass in the morning. The pioneers prepared supper over a campfire and then built the flames into a big bonfire and sang and danced together to forget their tiredness and the worries of the day.

Before each family went to its own wagon for the night, leaving only a guard on duty to watch for trouble of any kind, the whole group sang their song of encouragement to each other and of dedication to the Lord, "Come, Come, Ye Saints."

The old chief told the missionaries that on that evening he had with him over a thousand young braves, and each one was hidden behind a rock or tree with his bow and arrows ready to strike down the whole camp.

"I gave the signal," he said, "but our fingers were like stone. Not one arrow was shot. We mounted our horses and rode away because we knew the Great Spirit was watching over the pale faces."

The old chief took a violin from behind the door and started to play "Come, Come, Ye Saints." Then he stopped, looked intently at the missionaries, and finished his story. "This is your song, but it is my song too. I play it every night before I go to bed. It brings the Great Spirit here to me and makes me and my people calm and happy."

THE SHINING GIFT

The beautiful comb trimmed with shining stones that looked almost like diamonds was hidden safely waiting for Mother's Day. It had taken Robert months of hard work to earn enough money to make the purchase, but he knew his brother Nick had worked even longer and harder to buy the gift he had selected.

Though their mother worked hard, there was never money for the pretty things she loved. Father had told her the boys were planning a surprise. Robert thought he saw in her eyes the dream of something beautiful, and he knew the comb had been a perfect choice.

Nick had asked Robert not to give his gift until the right moment came. That moment arrived on the evening before Mother's Day when their mother got out her old scrub bucket and began to clean the shabby kitchen floor. Nick nodded to Robert, and then they ran to the secret place where their gifts were hidden.

Nick returned first, proudly carrying his present into the kitchen—a new scrub bucket with a wringer. A sad look came to mother's face when she saw it. Then she quickly tried to hide her disappointment

and started to thank Nick, but he had seen her disappointment and picked up the bucket and ran from the
room. Robert fingered the comb in his pocket. It
didn't seem the right time to give a beautiful gift, so
he followed his brother outside.

Just then their father came home. Nick's eyes
were filled with tears as he told of Mother's disappointment. "I'll take the bucket back to the store," he
sobbed.

"No," said Father. "Your gift is a clever one. I
wish I'd thought of it myself. Let's take it back to
Mother," and he led the boys into the kitchen where
Mother sat quietly staring at the floor. She did not
look up at first, then she wearily put out a hand for
the bucket and said, "It's a fine gift, son. Thank you."

"Oh, but Nick didn't explain about the gift," said
Father. "The most important part is that he'll scrub
half the floor whenever you use his bucket. Isn't that
so, Nick?"

Although Nick had not thought of this, he nodded
in agreement. Mother's eyes lighted up, and her
smile brightened the room.

Father turned to Robert. "And what is your gift
for Mother?"

Robert felt the comb in his pocket, the stones
rough against his fingers—shining stones almost
like diamonds. His gift was so beautiful, he thought,
that it would make the scrub bucket look even worse
by comparison.

After only a moment's hesitation, Robert turned
to Mother and said, "Why, half the pail is my gift,
and half the time I'll help Nick with the floor."

Mother's smile of understanding made the old
kitchen seem beautiful. Nick's eyes held so much
gratitude that Robert thought they shone even
brighter than the stones in the comb.

Topical Index